AQA STUDY GU

GCSE 9–1
THE SIGN OF
FOUR

BY ARTHUR CONAN DOYLE

SCHOLASTIC

Author Marie Lallaway

Series Consultants Richard Durant and Cindy Torn

Reviewer Rob Pollard

Editorial team Rachel Morgan, Audrey Stokes, Camilla Erskine, Lesley Densham, Anne Henwood, Caroline Low

Typesetting Oxford Designers & Illustrators Ltd

Cover design Nicolle Thomas and Neil Salt

App development Hannah Barnett, Phil Crothers and Haremi Ltd

Acknowledgements

Illustration Susan Szecsi/Oxford Designers & Illustrators

Photographs page 12: pocket watch, Yulia Glam; page 21: Votes for Women, HultonArchive/GettyImages; page 29: Regent Street, Lord Price Collection/Alamy; page 32: ornate keyhole, Chones/Shutterstock; page 38: police sign, Tony Bagget/Shutterstock; page 44: urchins, KGPA Ltd/Alamy; page 56: map of British Empire, Pictures Now/Alamy; page 60: Cuban Palm, Hein Nouwens/Shutterstock; page 61: British Soldiers defending Marzoline/Shutterstock; page 62: shilling, Ian Sanders/Alamy; page 72: Queen Victoria, Shutterstock/Everett Historical; page 73: Sikh Soldiers, Historic Collection/Alamy; page 74: image from Thrilling Life Stories for the Masses, Classic Collection/Alamy; page 80: Conan Doyle, Everett Historical/Shutterstock; magnifying glass, Yulia Glam/Shutterstock; page 90: girl doing exam, Monkey Business Images/Shutterstock; page 91: notepad and pen, TRINACRIA PHOTO/Shutterstock

Designed using Adobe InDesign

Published by Scholastic Education, an imprint of Scholastic Ltd, Book End, Range Road, Witney, Oxfordshire, OX29 0YD
Registered office: Westfield Road, Southam, Warwickshire CV47 0RA
www.scholastic.co.uk

Printed by Bell and Bain
© 2019 Scholastic Ltd
1 2 3 4 5 6 7 8 9 9 0 1 2 3 4 5 6 7 8

British Library Cataloguing-in-Publication Data
A catalogue record for this book is available from the British Library.

ISBN 978-1407-18266-7

Contents

**Check your answers on
the free revision app or at
www.scholastic.co.uk/gcse**

How to use
this book

This Study Guide is designed to help you prepare effectively for your AQA GCSE English literature exam question on *The Sign of Four* (Paper 1, Section B).

The content has been organised in a sequence that builds confidence, and which will deepen your knowledge and understanding of the novel step by step. Therefore, it is best to work through this book in the order that it is presented.

HOW TO REVISE!

This Study Guide uses the Scholastic Classics edition.

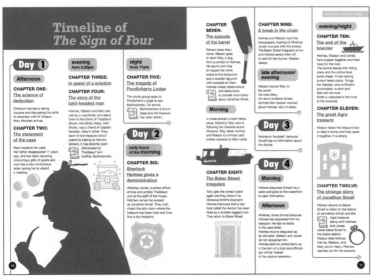

Know the plot

1 It is very important that you know the plot well: to be clear about what happens and in what order. The **timeline** on pages 10–11 provides a useful overview of the plot, highlighting key events.

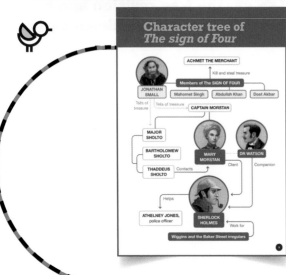

The **character tree** on page 9 introduces you to the main characters of the text.

The chronological section

2 The chronological section on pages 12–63 takes you through the novel scene by scene, providing plot summaries and pointing out important details. It is also designed to help you think about the structure of the novel.

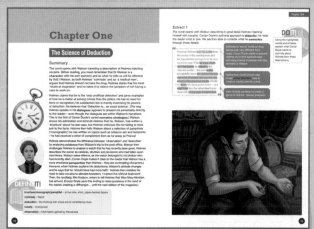

This section provides an in-depth exploration of themes or character development, drawing your attention to how Conan Doyle's language choices reveal the novel's meaning.

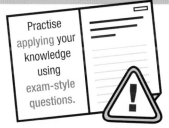

Practise applying your knowledge using exam-style questions.

The novel as a whole

3 The second half of the guide is retrospective: it helps you to look back over the whole novel through a number of relevant 'lenses': characters, themes, Conan Doyle's language, forms and structural features.

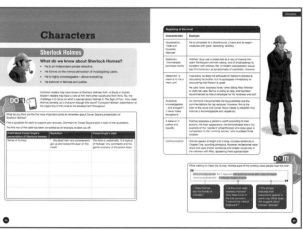

Doing well in your AQA exam

Stick to the **TIME LIMITS** you will need to in the exam.

4 Finally, you will find an extended 'Doing well in your AQA exam' section which guides you through the process of understanding questions, and planning and writing answers.

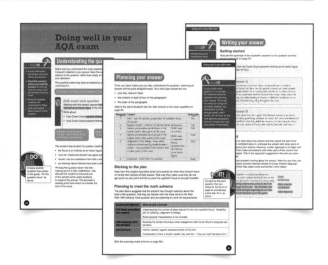

5

Features of this guide

The best way to retain information is to take an active approach to revision.

Throughout this book, you will find lots of features that will make your revision an active, successful process.

SNAPIT!

Use the Snap it! feature in the revision app to take pictures of key concepts and information. Great for revision on the go!

DEFINEIT!

Explains the meaning of difficult words from the set texts.

Callouts Additional explanations of important points.

words shown in **purple bold** can be found in the glossary on pages 94–95

Find methods of relaxation that work for you throughout the revision period.

Regular exercise helps stimulate the brain and will help you relax.

DOIT!

Activities to embed your knowledge and understanding and prepare you for the exams.

NAILIT!

Succinct and vital tips on how to do well in your exam.

STRETCHIT!

Provides content that stretches you further.

REVIEW IT!

Helps you to consolidate and understand what you have learned before moving on.

Revise in pairs or small groups and deliver presentations on topics to each other.

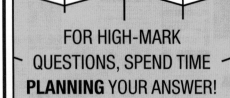

FOR HIGH-MARK QUESTIONS, SPEND TIME **PLANNING** YOUR ANSWER!

AQA exam-style question

AQA exam-style sample questions based on the extract shown are given on some pages. Use the sample mark scheme on page 86 to help you assess your responses. This will also help you understand what you could do to improve your response.

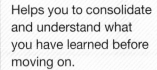

FREE REVISION APP

- The **free revision app** can be downloaded to your mobile phone (iOS and Android), making **on-the-go revision** easy.

- Use the revision calendar to help map out your revision in the lead-up to the exam.

- Complete multiple-choice questions and create your own **SNAP**IT! revision cards.

www.scholastic.co.uk/gcse

Online answers and additional resources

All of the tasks in this book are designed to get you thinking and to consolidate your understanding through thought and application. Therefore, it is important to write your own answers before checking. Some questions include tables where you need to fill in your answer in the book. Other questions require you to use a separate piece of paper so that you can draft your response and work out the best way of answering.

What do you learn about Holmes and Watson from this chapter? Collect any pieces of information about their physical appearance or background.

How does Conan Doyle want the reader to respond to Holmes' personality? Complete the table below – one example has been done for you.

Method	Quotation relating to Holmes	Reader's response
Dialogue – statement	'I abhor the dull routine of existence. I crave for mental exaltation.'	Reader could admire Holmes or think he is being arrogant.
Dialogue – statement	'I claim no credit in such cases. My name figures in no newspaper.'	
Description	'...leaning back luxuriously.... and sending up thick blue wreaths from his pipe.'	
Dialogue – interaction	'My dear doctor,' he said, kindly, 'pray accept my apologies.'	

Get plenty of sleep, especially the night before an exam.

LOOK AFTER YOURSELF

Help your brain by looking after your whole body!

Once you have worked through a section, you can check your answers to Do it!, Stretch it!, Review it! and the exam practice sections on the app or at **www.scholastic.co.uk/gcse**.

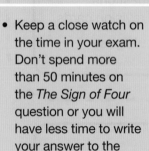

NAIL IT!

- Keep a close watch on the time in your exam. Don't spend more than 50 minutes on the *The Sign of Four* question or you will have less time to write your answer to the Shakespeare question in Section A.

- Take special care over spelling, punctuation and grammar as there are four extra marks available for these.

Why study *The Sign of Four*?

The Sign of Four, also called *The Sign of the Four*, Sir Arthur Conan Doyle's second novel, was originally written as a series for publication in Lippincott's Monthly Magazine in 1890. However, even before you read *The Sign of Four*, you are likely to have heard the name of Sherlock Holmes. Films and TV dramatisations are still being made of the original stories or of modern reinventions of the characters and plots.

The Victorian world of the novel is an essential backdrop to events. London is a fast-growing location and the River Thames is a source of work, transport and mystery. Victorian values, inventions and attitudes to the world may be vastly different from those of today, but the secret of good storytelling remains the same. Conan Doyle invites his readers to anticipate each stage of the story and enjoy the ingenuity of Sherlock Holmes as all the clues unite to uncover treasure and a villain…just as the most popular TV series do today.

The Sign of Four in your AQA exam

The Sign of Four is examined in Section B (the second half) of the first AQA GCSE English Literature exam, Paper 1 Shakespeare and 19th-century novel. Here is how it fits into the overall assessment framework:

Paper 1 Time: **1 hour 45 minutes**	Paper 2 Time: **2 hours 15 minutes**
Section A: Shakespeare	Section A: Modern prose or drama
Section B: 19th-century novel: *The Sign of Four*	Section B: Poetry anthology
	Section C: Unseen poetry

There will be just **one question** on *The Sign of Four* and you should not answer questions on any other 19th-century novel. Just answer the *The Sign of Four* question. You should spend **50 minutes** planning and writing your answer to the question. There are 30 marks available for the 19th-century novel question.

The 19th-century novel question will come with a short extract from the novel printed on the exam paper. You will find the question straight after the extract. The question will focus on character and/or theme. You must answer the question in relation to the extract and to relevant other parts of the novel that you have chosen.

A character tree

The 'character tree' on page 9 should help you to fix in your mind the names of the characters, their relationships and who did what to whom.

Timeline of *The Sign of Four*

The timeline on pages 10–11 provides a visual overview of the plot, highlighting key events which take place over the course of the novel. It will also help you to think about the structure of the novel.

Character tree of *The sign of Four*

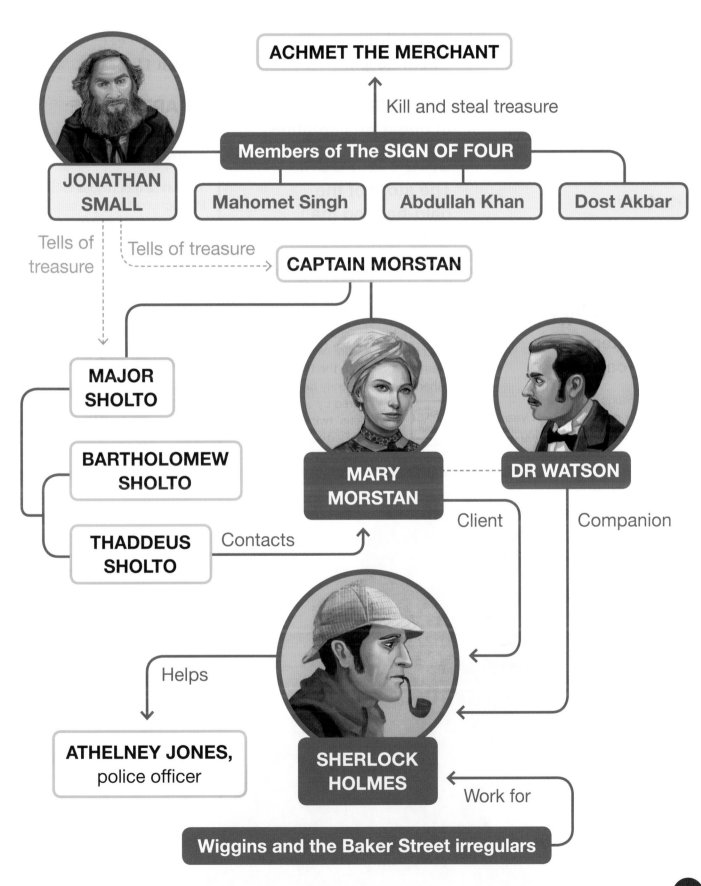

ACHMET THE MERCHANT

Kill and steal treasure

Members of The SIGN OF FOUR

JONATHAN SMALL

Mahomet Singh

Abdullah Khan

Dost Akbar

Tells of treasure

Tells of treasure

CAPTAIN MORSTAN

MAJOR SHOLTO

BARTHOLOMEW SHOLTO

THADDEUS SHOLTO

Contacts

MARY MORSTAN

DR WATSON

Client

Companion

Helps

SHERLOCK HOLMES

ATHELNEY JONES, police officer

Work for

Wiggins and the Baker Street irregulars

Timeline of *The Sign of Four*

Day 1

Afternoon

CHAPTER ONE:
The science of deduction

Sherlock Holmes is taking cocaine and discussing the skills of detection with Dr Watson. Mary Morstan arrives.

CHAPTER TWO:
The statement of the case

Mary explains her case. Her father disappeared 11 years ago, she has been receiving anonymous gifts of pearls and now has a new anonymous letter asking her to attend a meeting.

evening
from 5.50pm

CHAPTER THREE:
In quest of a solution

CHAPTER FOUR:
The story of the bald-headed man

Holmes, Watson and Mary are met by a coachman who takes them to the home of Thaddeus Sholto. His father, Major John Sholto, was a friend of Captain Morstan, Mary's father. They learn of lost treasure (which seems to belong to the two fathers). It has recently been discovered by Thaddeus' twin brother, Bartholomew.

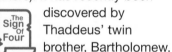

night
from 11pm

CHAPTER FIVE:
The tragedy of Pondicherry Lodge

The whole group goes to Pondicherry Lodge to see Bartholomew. On arrival,  Bartholomew is found dead and the treasure has been stolen.

Day 2

early hours of the **morning**

CHAPTER SIX:
Sherlock Holmes gives a demonstration

Athelney Jones, a police officer, arrives and arrests Thaddeus and all the staff of the house. Holmes names his suspect as Jonathan Small. They both check the attic room where the treasure had been kept and they find a tiny footprint.

CHAPTER SEVEN:
The episode of the barrel

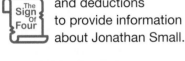

Watson takes Mary home. Watson goes to fetch Toby, a dog, from a contact of Holmes. He returns and they re-inspect the crime scene to find footprints and a wooden-leg print with creosote on them. Holmes makes observations and deductions to provide information about Jonathan Small.

Morning

A chase across London takes place, following Toby who is following the creosote scent. However, Toby takes Holmes and Watson to a timber yard (where creosote is often used).

Aurora

CHAPTER EIGHT:
The Baker Street irregulars

Toby gets the correct scent again and they follow it to Mordecai Smith's boatyard. Holmes discovers that a fast boat called the *Aurora* has been hired by a wooden-legged man. They return to Baker Street.

221B

CHAPTER NINE:
A break in the chain

Holmes and Watson read the newspapers, hearing of Athelney Jones' success with the arrests. The Baker Street Irregulars arrive and Holmes sends them off to look for the *Aurora*. Watson sleeps.

late afternoon/ evening

Watson returns Toby to his owner.
He visits Mary.
On return to Baker Street, he finds Mrs Hudson worried about Holmes' lack of sleep.

Day 3

Holmes is 'troubled' because he still has no information about the *Aurora*.

Day 4

Morning

Holmes disguises himself as a sailor and goes to the waterfront to seek information.

Afternoon

Athelney Jones arrives because Holmes has requested him via telegram. He has no leads in the case either.
Holmes returns disguised as an old sailor. Watson and Jones do not recognise him.
Holmes asks for police back-up in the form of a boat and officers but will be 'master' of the capture operation.

evening/night

CHAPTER TEN:
The end of the Islander

Holmes, Watson and Jones have supper together and then head for the river.
The *Aurora* leaves the hiding place and the police boat gives chase. A hair-raising pursuit takes place. Tonga, the Islander, who is Small's accomplice, is shot and falls into the river.
Small is captured in the mud of the riverside.

CHAPTER ELEVEN:
The great Agra treasure

Watson takes the treasure box to Mary's home and they open it together. It is empty.

CHAPTER TWELVE:
The strange story of Jonathan Small

Watson returns to Baker Street to listen to the history of Johnathan Small and the Agra treasure, along with Holmes and Jones.
Jones takes Small to the police station.
Watson tells Holmes that he, Watson, and Mary are to marry. Holmes reaches out for his cocaine.

Chapter One

The Science of Deduction

Summary

The novel opens with Watson narrating a description of Holmes injecting cocaine. (When reading, you must remember that Dr Watson is a **character** with his own opinions and so what he tells us will be affected by that.) Watson, as both Holmes' 'comrade' and as 'a medical man', argues that Holmes should not take the drug. Holmes states that his mind 'rebels at stagnation' and he takes it to relieve the boredom of not having a case to work on.

Holmes claims that he is the 'only unofficial detective' and gives examples of how he is better at solving crimes than the police. He has no need for fame or recognition; his satisfaction lies in merely exercising his powers of detection. He believes that 'Detection is…an exact science'. (The way Holmes speaks in his **dialogues** appears to present his personality directly to the reader – even though the dialogues are within Watson's narrations. This is the first of Conan Doyle's varied **narrative strategies**.) Watson shows his admiration and reminds Holmes that he, Watson, had written a 'brochure' about his last case, but Holmes criticises this for failing to stick just to the facts. Holmes then tells Watson about a selection of pamphlets ('monographs') he has written on topics such as tobacco ash and footprints – he has received a letter of compliment from as far away as France!

Holmes demonstrates the difference between 'observation' and 'deduction' by analysing **evidence** from Watson's trip to the post office. Watson then challenges Holmes to analyse a watch that he has recently been given. Holmes describes the owner as careless, drunken and someone who had fallen upon hard times. Watson takes offence, as the watch belonged to his brother who had recently died. (Conan Doyle makes it clear to the reader that Watson has a more emotional **perspective** than Holmes – they are contrasting characters.) However, when Holmes explains his deductions, Watson's attitude changes and he says that he 'should have had more faith'. Holmes then restates his need to take cocaine to alleviate boredom, 'I cannot live without brainwork'. Then, the landlady, Mrs Hudson, enters to tell Holmes that Miss Mary Morstan has arrived. (Conan Doyle uses this ending to raise questions in the mind of the reader, creating a cliffhanger… until the next edition of the magazine.)

DEFINE IT!

brochure/monograph/pamphlet – at the time, short, paper-backed books

comrade – friend

deduction – the thinking that arises out of considering clues

faculty – brainpower

observation – information gained by the senses

Extract 1

The novel opens with Watson describing in great detail Holmes injecting himself with cocaine. Conan Doyle's authorial approach is **didactic**: he 'tells' the reader what to see. We are then able to consider what he **connotes** through these details.

> Sherlock Holmes took his bottle from the corner of the mantelpiece and his hypodermic syringe from its neat morocco case. With his long, white,
> 5 nervous fingers he adjusted the delicate needle…his eyes rested thoughtfully upon the sinewy forearm and wrist all dotted and scarred with innumerable puncture-marks. Finally
> 10 he thrust the sharp point home…and sank back into the velvet-lined arm-chair with a long sigh of satisfaction.

Attitudes to 'social' levels of drug-taking were very different from today. Conan Doyle wants to present Holmes as a more sophisticated and experimental character than the sensible Dr Watson.

Notice how Conan Doyle uses longer **noun phrases** here to create a visually precise scene.

Verb choices combine to create a sense of Holmes' relaxed precision.

DO IT!

Using the highlighted words and phrases, explain what Conan Doyle wants to connote about Holmes from these descriptions.

DO IT!

Explain the **language** highlighted in yellow in the extract in your own words.

What might Conan Doyle want to connote about Holmes by having him speak in this way?

STRETCH IT!

How do these **quotations** show that Holmes is in control of the situation and himself here? How is Watson presented as a **foil** in this scene?

DEFINE IT!

Afghan campaign – battles in Afghanistan in 1878–80

brusquely – sharply

clarifying to the mind – makes you think clearly

constitution – health

languidly – without hurrying

small moment – little importance

transcendentally stimulating – causing ecstasy, taking your mind out of itself

vehemence – strength or intensity of feeling

Extract 2

Watson and Holmes talk about Holmes' drug-taking. Watson is presented as a foil to Holmes. His attitudes are very different.

> 'Which is it today?' I asked, 'morphine or cocaine?'
> He raised his eyes languidly from the old black-letter volume which he had
> 5   opened.
> 'It is cocaine,' he said, 'a seven-per-cent solution. Would you care to try it?'
> 'No, indeed,' I answered, brusquely. 'My constitution has not got over the Afghan
> 10 campaign yet. I cannot afford to throw any extra strain upon it.'
> He smiled at my vehemence. 'Perhaps you are right, Watson,' he said. 'I suppose that its influence is
> 15 physically a bad one. I find it, however, so transcendently stimulating and clarifying to the mind that its secondary action is a matter of small moment.'

Watson's questions are used as a **narrative device** throughout the novel to prompt Holmes to give information.

Holmes is always presented as being relaxed and in control.

The **dialogue** allows us to learn how Holmes speaks. He uses **elevated vocabulary**.

Character and theme essentials

Context

The Victorian world was quite different to our own. It was normal for middle-class gentleman to share and rent rooms or a floor of a house, and Mrs Hudson behaves as both home-owner and in a servant role to Holmes and Watson.

With the growth of the Empire (see page 72), substances from countries abroad made their way to England, and taking drugs would have been considered in a similar way to having a drink or a smoke – though perhaps somewhat more interesting. Smoking was not seen as a health risk and Conan Doyle probably intended Holmes' drug taking as a sign of his masculinity.

Communication was either verbal, mostly face-to-face with relatively little use of the telephone (Athelney Jones uses the telephone only once in this novel), or written on paper. There was no electricity, radio, television or internet. So, the circulation of ideas was through 'pamphlets', books and newspapers. The fact that Holmes' work had been read in France would have been considered important or ground-breaking.

NAILIT!

When you write about a character in the exam, remember that they are the creation of the author, Conan Doyle, and do not exist as real people.

Character

First impressions count. Conan Doyle uses description, dialogue and character interaction to present his characters.

DOIT!

What do you learn about Holmes and Watson from this chapter? Collect any pieces of information about their physical appearance or background.

How does Conan Doyle want the reader to respond to Holmes' personality? Complete the table below – one example has been done for you.

Method	Quotation relating to Holmes	Reader's response
Dialogue – statement	'I abhor the dull routine of existence. I crave for mental exaltation.'	Reader could admire Holmes or think he is being arrogant.
Dialogue – statement	'I claim no credit in such cases. My name figures in no newspaper.'	
Description	'…leaning back luxuriously… and sending up thick blue wreaths from his pipe.'	
Dialogue – interaction	'My dear doctor,' he said, kindly, 'pray accept my apologies.'	

 STRETCH**IT!**

How do Watson and Holmes interact? Support your opinions with brief examples from the text.

REVIEW IT!

1 Who is narrating?

2 What is Holmes doing at the start of the novel?

3 He does this because he 'rebels at stagnation'. What does this mean?

4 What is Watson's attitude to this? What does this show about the relationship?

5 Who is Athelney Jones?

6 Who, according to Holmes, are usually 'out of their depths'?

7 Give two facts about Watson.

8 What is a monograph?

9 'You have an extraordinary genius for minutiae.' Who does this comment refer to and what does it mean?

10 According to Holmes, 'Detection is, or ought to be,' what?

11 How does Holmes know that Watson has been to the post office? Is this an example of observation or deduction?

12 How does Holmes know that Watson sent a telegram?

13 What is the test that Watson sets Holmes?

14 Who was the owner of the watch before Watson?

15 How does Watson respond to what Holmes says about his brother?

16 Why has Conan Doyle included this test as part of the first chapter?

17 What does this particular test show about the relationship between Watson and Holmes?

18 Who is Mrs Hudson?

19 Name the guest who has arrived.

20 Holmes or Watson: who do you prefer at this point in the novel, and why?

Chapter Two

The Statement of the Case

Summary

Mary Morstan enters. Watson's admiration for her is evident in his flattering description. Holmes is polite, placing a seat for her, but businesslike: 'State your case.' (Conan Doyle now shows Holmes in action as a detective to contrast with the previous chapter.) Mary explains the mystery of her father, Captain Morstan, who disappeared on the night that he had arranged to meet her in London. She had been separated from him while he worked as soldier in the Andaman Islands. (She had been sent to England for her education because her mother was dead.)

Holmes asks direct questions: 'The date?...Had he any friends in town?' Captain Morstan's friend in England had been Major Sholto, but Mary had come to a dead end as to what may have happened to her father.

Four years later, she had seen an advertisement from someone asking for her address. She had replied and since then had anonymously been sent a valuable pearl. Her reason for coming to see Holmes was because she had received a further letter instructing her to meet in person – along with two of her companions. (The author has selected components for a detective novel: a disappearance, valuable jewels, a mysterious benefactor, an anonymous note. Conan Doyle was one of the first writers in the detective **fiction** genre.)

Holmes and Mary ask Watson to attend this meeting with them. Holmes inspects the handwriting, which he states has been disguised. Mary leaves and Watson comments, 'What a very attractive woman!' Holmes, however, sees her as a 'mere unit'. Holmes goes out and leaves Watson romanticising about Mary. (This relationship gives the novel a **sub-plot** to vary focus from the main detection **plot**, providing the reader with a different kind of entertainment – and, possibly, to appeal to a wider readership.)

DO IT!

1 How does Holmes' use of **aphorisms** add to his characterisation?

2 It is easy to see Sherlock Holmes as 'inhuman' and without emotions. Scan the first two chapters to find examples of his more humane qualities such as kindness and care for others.

STRETCH IT!

Does Sherlock Holmes have a social conscience (a sense of responsibility or concern for the injustices of society)? Is he, in fact, a philanthropist?

Explain your answer using evidence from the first two chapters.

Mary Morstan

The description of Mary is balanced: she is not a sensational character. Her appearance is attractive, but in moderation. She has 'the most perfect taste' even though she is of 'limited means'; she stands out in the crowd with the 'white feather' in her hat. Watson's attraction is clear.

Look at Mary's reactions:
- She has an 'outward composure of manner'.
- 'her lip trembled, her hand quivered…'
- She gives a 'bright, kindly glance'.
- She answers Holmes' questions with certainty and presents him with the letter.

How far is Mary presented as a helpless female? Explain your answer.

STRETCH IT!

Holmes sees Mary as a 'mere unit' rather than an 'attractive woman'. How does this affect our view of Holmes? Is he sexist in this instance? Explain your thoughts.

Extract 1

Watson watches Mary leave and talks to Holmes.

"
Standing at the window, I watched her walking briskly down the street, until the grey turban and white feather were but a speck in the
5 sombre crowd.
'What a very attractive woman!' I exclaimed, turning to my companion. He had lit his pipe again, and was leaning back with drooping eyelids.
10 'Is she?' he said, languidly. 'I did not observe.'
'You really are an automaton, – a calculating-machine!' I cried. 'There is something positively inhuman in
15 you at times.'
He smiled gently. 'It is of the first importance,' he said, 'not to allow your judgment to be biased by personal qualities. A client is to me a
20 mere unit, a factor in a problem. The emotional qualities are antagonistic to clear reasoning. I assure you that the most winning woman I ever knew was hanged for poisoning three little
25 children for their insurance-money, and the most repellent man of my acquaintance is a philanthropist who has spent nearly a quarter of a million upon the London poor.'
30 'In this case, however—'
'I never make exceptions. An exception disproves the rule.'
"

DEFINE IT!

antagonistic – working against

automaton – robot

inhuman – uncaring, unemotional

philanthropist – a person who does good for others

sombre – here, it means dull and serious

unit – item of data

winning woman – attractive woman

Notice how Mary's hat makes her stand out from the crowd in both Watson's eyes and our own.

Conan Doyle frequently gives highly **visual** presentations of **settings**.

Notice how Holmes is a **foil** to Watson in this scene. This scene emphasises the contrast between Holmes, and Watson's reactions to people. Watson is presented as more emotional and Holmes as clinical and detached. Look out for other examples of this throughout the novel.

Ironically, Watson accuses Holmes of being 'inhuman' but Holmes proves that his logic is, in fact, humane and he does not judge people by their outward appearances.

Look out for other examples of Holmes' behaviour with people of different appearances, classes and backgrounds.

Holmes controls the dialogue once again. However, Conan Doyle has used this short sentence to make Holmes seem less arrogant than he otherwise might do. Why do you think Conan Doyle has done this?

Throughout the novel, Holmes states a variety of **aphorisms**.

Character and theme essentials

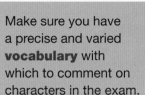

NAILIT!

Make sure you have a precise and varied **vocabulary** with which to comment on characters in the exam.

Women

Conan Doyle is a product of his time and the prevailing attitudes towards women are evident in his novels. The Victorian era, like many periods of time before and after it, was a time of misogyny (prejudice against women). Middle-class women had particular roles in the house and family. Women did not have the right to vote and were seen as 'less' than men in terms of their ability to think. They were expected to be emotional and dependent upon a man for guidance. Mary fulfils some of these stereotypical views, but Conan Doyle has also given her enough character to make her important and genuinely interesting within the novel. Watson is attracted to her and this brings out his more sensitive side, in contrast to Holmes' detachment.

Watson reflects, 'In an experience of women which extends over many nations and three separate continents, I have never looked upon a face which gave a clearer promise of a refined and sensitive nature.' (Notice here how it is Watson who makes a judgement – he has the power to decide. It also sounds as if he assesses all women, based mainly upon their appearance, and puts them in a rank order. The qualities mentioned here are submissive and emotional. Conan Doyle is trying to pay a compliment to Mary here, but it may sound sexist to us today.)

Holmes, Watson, Mary Morstan

Mary begins the novel as a relatively dynamic character – making the decision to contact Holmes, showing strength through the difficulties in her past, and then accompanying Holmes and Watson on the visit to Pondicherry Lodge. However, by the end of the novel she is presented sentimentally, framed in a window, ready to accept Watson's proposal.

On first meeting Mary, Holmes is conventionally polite but business-like. Although a little apprehensive, Mary is presented as purposeful and logical, qualities that Holmes later compliments her upon when talking to Watson about marriage. Holmes is never critical of Mary and he acknowledges Watson's affection for her when arranging with the police that Watson should open the treasure chest with her (rather than the police themselves opening it). Holmes is critical of Watson's desire to marry, regarding it as needless; however, he only ever treats Mary with respect, even though to him, as a client, she is a 'mere unit'.

Watson is immediately attracted to Mary and his affections form the sub-plot to the novel. He focuses on her facial appearance and compliments her tasteful choice of clothes. At each stage of the novel, Watson expresses protectiveness towards Mary, which increases as the plot develops; this can actually make Mary seem less capable as the novel progresses. At the end, the reader, along with Watson and Mary, enjoy the fact that the romantic couple has found their own 'treasure' in each other and a marriage is announced.

Which of these adjectives would you apply to Holmes, Watson and Mary in this chapter? Link each one you choose with a specific example from Chapter Two. Some have been done for you.

analytical   assertive   considerate   critical   detached   eager
independent   romantic   regretful   superior   sentimental

Holmes	Watson	Mary

Detached	Sentimental	Assertive
He ignores Mary's sobs and goes straight in with his questions.	*His description of Mary is idealistic.*	*She takes charge of her life by finding a solution to her dilemma of meeting the unknown man by asking Holmes for help.*

REVIEW IT!

1 According to Watson's description, Mary Morstan:

 a is small and dainty.

 b is dressed quite simply.

 c has beautiful brown hair.

 d wears a feather in her hat.

 (Circle all that apply.)

2 "In an experience of women which extends over many nations and three separate continents, I have never looked upon a face which gave a clearer promise of a refined and sensitive nature."

 Why has Watson included this information about himself? Give two reasons.

3 Why has Mary chosen to come to Holmes?

4 What do Mrs Forrester's comments show us about Holmes?

5 Holmes has 'clear-cut, hawklike features'. Why has Conan Doyle chosen to compare Holmes to a hawk?

For questions 6–10, complete the summary of Mary's history.

6 Mary's mother _____ when she was young.

7 Mary's father sent her to _____ to be cared for while he remained an officer in an _____ regiment of the army.

8 When Mary was _____, her father took _____ months' leave and returned to _____.

9 Mary's father telegraphed her from _____ and invited her to come to see him. When she arrived, he was _____. He had not been seen since the _____ morning.

10 After waiting for _____ day, Mary contacted _____ and advertised in the _____ to try to find him.

11 Mary ends her account with a sob. What does Holmes do next?

12 What does this show about him?

13 Why does Mary put her own address in *The Times* newspaper?

14 What is in the box?

15 Why has Mary come to see Holmes today?

16 In what ways is the letter typical of a detective novel device?

17 Although Watson finds Mary very attractive, he tries not to think about her. Why?

18 'A client is to me a mere unit.' How does Holmes' reaction differ from Watson's?

19 Conan Doyle has chosen to show Mary walking 'briskly' down the street. What does this small detail show about her character?

20 At the end of the chapter, Watson thinks 'She was a unit, a factor – nothing more.' Why has Conan Doyle chosen to have Watson echo Holmes' words?

Chapter Three: In Quest of a Solution

Summary

Holmes returns 'in excellent spirits' later in the afternoon. He had been looking through past copies of *The Times* to find that Major Sholto had died. (Libraries or newspaper offices would have kept old copies of newspapers for research purposes. Remember – there was no internet or any form of electronic data storage. Thus, Holmes must have researched with considerable speed and concentration.)

Within weeks of Major Sholto's death, the advertisement appeared and Mary had started to receive the pearls as gifts. Holmes **deduces** that Sholto's heir is involved and is making compensation linked to her father's death. Although he cannot explain the whole case, Holmes is confident that the meeting will enlighten him.

Mary arrives in a 'four-wheeler', Watson picks up his 'heaviest stick' and Holmes 'his revolver'. Mary tells of a 'curious paper' found in her father's desk. She shows it to Holmes, who observes that the paper is 'of native Indian manufacture', and he recites the names written on it: 'The sign of the four – Jonathan Small, Mahomet Singh, Abdullah Khan, Dost Akbar.' (Victorian England was less ethnically mixed. Think about the effect of 'exotic' names upon a readership that considered England as the 'centre' of their world.)

They set off across London to their meeting place in front of the Lyceum Theatre. They are met by a 'small, dark, brisk man' who takes them in another carriage out of the city. Holmes recites the street names as they go.

When they arrive, the door of the house is opened by a 'Hindoo servant' wearing a turban. A strange voice instructs the group to enter.

STRETCH IT!

Why does Conan Doyle restate information already known to the reader? How does this affect the reader?

Further character information is being provided all the time.

Name the character each quotation below refers to: Holmes, Watson or Mary.

Is the information new, or does it restate something already known from the first chapter?

Quotation	Which character?	What is **implied** by this information?	New or old information? If old, give a previous reference to this.
has 'fits of the blackest depression'			
'said…pensively'			
'nervous and depressed'			
'as resolute and collected as ever'			
'never at fault'			

DEFINE IT!

memoranda – notes

petty – here: small, unnecessary

pocket-lantern – (before batteries and torches were invented) a small lantern lit with a flame

thoroughfare – road

DO IT!

1 Holmes is presented as unemotional in this extract.

a Can you find any other examples of this from the chapters you have read so far?

b Why has Conan Doyle emphasised this difference between Holmes and other characters such as Watson and Mary?

2 Explain how Conan Doyle uses pathetic fallacy in extract 1 to convey Watson's mood.

Extract 1

Watson gives a description and shares his thoughts about the London streets as the group travel through the city. Conan Doyle uses **pathetic fallacy** to combine the weather and the emotional mood of the characters. This description of light and gloom could possibly be an **analogy** for Watson's emotions.

"
It was a September evening, and not yet seven o'clock, but the day had been a dreary one, and a dense drizzly fog lay low upon the great city.
5 Mud-coloured clouds drooped sadly over the muddy streets. Down the Strand the lamps were but misty splotches of diffused light which threw a feeble circular glimmer upon
10 the slimy pavement. The yellow glare from the shop-windows streamed out into the steamy, vaporous air, and threw a murky, shifting radiance across the crowded thoroughfare.
15 There was, to my mind, something eerie and ghost-like in the endless procession of faces which flitted across these narrow bars of light, – sad faces and glad, haggard and
20 merry. Like all human kind, they flitted from the gloom into the light, and so back into the gloom once more. I am not subject to impressions, but the dull, heavy
25 evening, with the strange business upon which we were engaged, combined to make me nervous and depressed. I could see from Miss Morstan's manner that she was
30 suffering from the same feeling. Holmes alone could rise superior to petty influences. He held his open notebook upon his knee, and from time to time he jotted down figures
35 and memoranda in the light of his pocket-lantern.
"

The adjectives used to describe the scene are all 'negative' and describe dampened colours. Notice how **consonance** using the letter 'd' creates a heavy feeling to the words.

The **sibilant** 's' words have a weakness to their sound that shows how ineffectually the light pierces the dull skyscape.

Watson's observations imply his character. Would you agree that this extract could suggest that he is observant, reflective, serious, melancholy, sensitive and perhaps overly dramatic?

Notice how Watson, and Conan Doyle, separate Holmes from experiencing the same emotions as others.

STRETCH IT!

In extract 1, could Watson's description of the movement of people, 'they flitted from the gloom into the light, and so back into the gloom once more' be seen as an **analogy** to his emotional experience since meeting Mary? Explain your opinion.

Chapter Four: The Story of the Bald-headed Man

Summary

Holmes, Watson and Mary enter an exotically furnished apartment. They meet Thaddeus Sholto. He is small and bald with a high voice and yellow teeth. Thaddeus tells Mary about treasure she is entitled to (through her father) that has finally been located in a secret room at Pondicherry Lodge, the home of Brother Bartholomew. (Flashback: Notice how Conan Doyle toys with the reader's curiosity by pausing the progress of the detection plot. Here, he delays the action by inserting an explanation. Look out for other examples of this.)

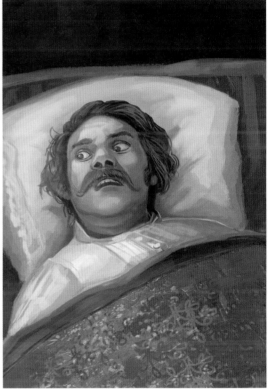

Thaddeus tells the story of his father, Major John Sholto – who never went out alone, and feared wooden-legged men. He had retired from the Indian Army with wealth, servants and 'a large collection of valuables'. When Morstan disappeared, Major Sholto was unconcerned, despite Morstan being a close friend from India.

One day, a letter had arrived from India that gave the major a shock and he had 'sickened to his death'. Close to dying, he gave his sons a true account of Morstan's death. (This idea of becoming ill or dying from the trauma of a shock was more realistic to a Victorian reader than it may appear to you.)

Further flashback: Morstan had visited to claim his share of the treasure. They had argued, Morstan had suffered a heart attack, had fallen, bashing his head, and had died. Lal Chowdar, the servant, assumed Major Sholto had killed him and they disposed of the body.

Near death, the major wished to ensure that Mary would receive her father's share of the treasure. When just about to tell his secret, a face 'with wild cruel eyes' appeared at the window. This had shocked the major and he died. A single footprint was found outside the window…and a note signed with 'The sign of the four'.

Mary is 'deadly white' with shock. Holmes' eyes are 'glittering'. They leave for Pondicherry Lodge but Watson is downhearted because Mary will become a wealthy heiress (any chance of marriage would become impossible because of their differences in social station). (Notice how Conan Doyle uses journey times to give Watson opportunities for comment. This adds variety to how the plot is **structured**.)

DO IT!

Conan Doyle uses a range of narrative devices to structure his novel, offering the reader an engaging variety. Which methods can you identify in this chapter?

monologue   dialogue   **reflective commentary** description

change of direction   comedy   enigmatic information   action sequence

Extract 1

Thaddeus Sholto untactfully tells Mary that her father is dead, before explaining the difficulty of approaching Brother Bartholomew about sharing the treasure.

Conan Doyle's mastery of plot is shown here. Captain Morstan's death is announced so that a reader's focus is transferred to how and why he died.

Here, Conan Doyle develops Watson's characterisation, showing him as a protector and gentleman but also capable of violence.

The precision of phrasing draws attention to Mary's lips in a way that would be quite sensuous to the Victorian reader.

Brother Bartholomew is an enigmatic character. A sense of mystery is built up about him before we discover his role with the treasure and that he is Thaddeus' twin. Conan Doyle uses this as a **structural device**.

Conan Doyle often uses a string of adjectives like this to introduce characters or to remind a reader – remember that the novel was first published as a series. Here Thaddeus is presented as weak and vulnerable.

> 'Had your father, Miss Morstan, refrained from throwing a strain upon his heart, he might have been alive now.'
> I could have struck the man across the face,
> 5 so hot was I at this callous and off-hand reference to so delicate a matter. Miss Morstan sat down, and her face grew white to the lips.
> 'I knew in my heart that he was dead,' said
> 10 she.
> 'I can give you every information,' said he, 'and, what is more, I can do you justice; and I will, too, whatever Brother Bartholomew may say…The three of us can show a bold
> 15 front to Brother Bartholomew. But let us have no outsiders, – no police or officials… Nothing would annoy Brother Bartholomew more than any publicity.'
> He sat down upon a low settee and blinked
> 20 at us inquiringly with his weak, watery blue eyes.
> 'For my part,' said Holmes, 'whatever you may choose to say will go no further.'

As Holmes says in Chapter One, he is the 'only unofficial consulting detective' and the 'last and highest court of appeal in detection'. He often takes charge of the situation.

DOIT!

How does Conan Doyle explore the **theme** of justice through the character of Thaddeus Sholto?

- Does Thaddeus behave justly? What is the final consequence of this?
- Does Thaddeus receive justice during the novel? (Think about his interactions with Holmes and Athelney Jones.)
- Compare Thaddeus' behaviour and consequences with others in his family.

Write a short paragraph.

STRETCH IT!

Look back to Chapter Two where Holmes refers to the 'philanthropist' with a 'repellent' appearance. Make a link to this and Holmes' treatment of Thaddeus Sholto. Consider how Conan Doyle has presented Thaddeus Sholto in this chapter. Write a paragraph about Holmes' sense of justice to explore this link.

Character and theme essentials

Location

Conan Doyle ranges through a variety of locations across the novel. His descriptions of setting are usually quite brief but highly detailed.

In extract 1 on page 26, pathetic fallacy is used to create an emotional **tone** to reflect Watson's despondent mood. On other occasions, Conan Doyle favours precise, observational language to give a clear visual image of a scene. Cinemas did not exist when Conan Doyle was writing but his descriptions do have a cinematic vision. Imagine this scene in your mind's eye:

Extract 1

> A busy air is created by using a range of people and objects to populate the scene.

> Precise adjectives add the finer details and pick out points of reference for the reader.

> Verbs and adverbials provide the noise and movement.

> The imaginary 'camera' moves in for a closer look, picking out one person to contrast with the crowd.

> "At the Lyceum Theatre the crowds were already thick at the side-entrances. In front a continuous stream of hansoms and four-wheelers were rattling up, discharging their cargoes of shirt-fronted men
> 5 and beshawled, be-diamonded women. We had hardly reached the third pillar, which was our rendezvous, before a small, dark, brisk man in the dress of a coachman accosted us."

In extract 2, Conan Doyle refers to London streets. Even if the reader had never been to the city, the names of rows, squares, bridges and the river could be imagined, and the listing of them gives a sense of the urban sprawl and movement through it. Holmes' vast and useful knowledge is again demonstrated:

Extract 2

> "'Rochester Row,' said he. 'Now Vincent Square. Now we come out on the Vauxhall Bridge Road. We are making for the Surrey side, apparently. Yes, I thought so. Now we are on the bridge. You can catch glimpses of the river.'"

Remember to consider the novel from the perspective of a Victorian reader. Conan Doyle includes the London street names that would be familiar to some, but not to others. They give the novel a sense of location – perhaps in the same way that a cityscape sets the mood and scene for many of today's detective narratives. Think about why it is Holmes that gives this information in the narrative.

DO IT!

Go to the final paragraph of the chapter, beginning 'We had, indeed, reached…' Explore how Conan Doyle creates a negative impression of the neighbourhood. Pay particular attention to the **metaphor** of the city having 'monster tentacles'.

The Sholto family

Major John Sholto has twin sons, Thaddeus and Bartholomew. Major Sholto's actions have begun the series of events narrated in the novel. His greed is at fault. However, Thaddeus seems to represent a different kind of morality and behaviour. John and Bartholomew represent the selfish pursuit of greed; Thaddeus represents kindness and honour.

Identify which member of the Sholto family each comment or quotation relates to.

'a bristle of red hair all round the fringe of it, and a bald, shining scalp which shot out from among it like a mountain-peak from fir-trees.'

He is quick to anger and has a bad temper.

He is driven by greed.

He is called 'villain' and 'scoundrel'.

He is 'a little inclined to my father's fault'.

In death he has 'a horrible smile, a fixed and unnatural grin'.

'We were your trustees.'

'He writhed his hands together as he stood…'

He claims to be 'a great sufferer' and he avoids 'the crowd'.

He is benevolent and accepts moral responsibility for Mary's future.

He feels a 'cursed greed which has been my besetting sin through life'.

'An oasis of art in the howling desert of South London.'

'…had the helpless appealing expression of a terrified child.'

Chapter Three: In Quest of a Solution

1 What does Watson say about Holmes' moods?

2 Why has Conan Doyle created Holmes' character this way?

3 What research has Holmes been doing?

4 What has Holmes deduced from his research?

5 Mary Morstan arrives in a 'four-wheeler'. What is this?

6 'Our night's work might be a serious one'. What have Holmes and Watson taken with them?

7 Why has Conan Doyle included these details?

8 Mary is 'composed, but pale…her self-control was perfect'. Is this just Watson's attraction to Mary, or is Conan Doyle creating an assertive female character?

9 Where were Captain Morstan and Major Sholto based?

10 Mary says, 'By the way…' and explains that there had been a note in her father's possession. Why has Conan Doyle introduced the note *now* and not before?

11 'I begin to suspect that this matter may turn out to be much deeper and more subtle than I at first supposed. I must reconsider my ideas.' What does this tell us about Holmes?

12 Look at the section describing the city, beginning 'It was a September evening…' In what ways does this setting create a mood of expectation?

13 How do Watson and Mary feel about the 'strange business'? How does Holmes feel?

14 Mary gives her word that Holmes and Watson are not policemen. The coachman just accepts this. How do you respond to this situation?

15 How is the coach driven? How does this add to the reader's entertainment?

16 Conan Doyle chooses to include many street names. Why does he do this?

17 'Our quest does not appear to take us to very fashionable regions.' What does Holmes mean?

18 What do you learn about the development of London in the Victorian era from the description 'the monster tentacles which the giant city was throwing out into the country'?

19 Who opens the door and how is he dressed?

20 What is the impact of this upon the narrative?

Chapter Four: The Story of the Bald-headed Man

1 Give three details about Thaddeus Sholto from the opening paragraph of this chapter. What does Conan Doyle think of him?

2 Give three details of Sholto's apartment. In the **context** of the Victorian era, what reaction does Conan Doyle hope for from his readers?

3 What is a hookah? Why has it been included in the description?

4 What does Thaddeus Sholto ask Watson to do? Why has Conan Doyle included this detail?

5 Who 'could have struck the man across the face'? Why?

6 Brother Bartholomew is mentioned five times before we learn that he is Thaddeus' twin. What is the effect of repeating his name in this way?

7 Thaddeus Sholto tells of his art collection, but it is irrelevant to the plot. Why has Conan Doyle included this detail?

8 'You cannot imagine what a terrible fellow he is when he is angry.' What is the effect on the reader of knowing this about Bartholomew?

9 Why does the group not go to Pondicherry Lodge immediately? Why has Conan Doyle stalled the action at this point in the plot?

10 Complete this sentence: Major _____ Sholto retired from the Indian Army _____ years ago. He had _____ children.

11 How did Captain Morstan die?

12 Why did Major Sholto not tell the truth?

13 How does the servant, Lal Chowder, react to Morstan's death? How does this make him appear?

14 What stops Major Sholto from telling his sons where the treasure is?

15 Give three details from Major Sholto's death that increase the mystery at this point in the novel.

16 How does Mary Morstan react to this tale? Look back to her reaction to her father's death. Is Conan Doyle's presentation of Mary misogynistic (prejudiced against women)?

17 Mary says 'It was extremely good of you' to thank Thaddeus Sholto for sending the pearls to her. Why has Conan Doyle included this detail?

18 Conan Doyle offers a close-up portrait of Thaddeus Sholto preparing to leave the house. Remind yourself of this section and then explain why Conan Doyle has included this detail.

19 The treasure may be worth 'not less than half a million sterling'. Why is Watson disturbed by this? What does it tell you about society in the Victorian era?

20 Compare the ending of this chapter to the previous one. What similarity do you notice? Bearing in mind that he was writing for a magazine series, why might Conan Doyle have used this **technique**?

Chapter Five

The Tragedy of Pondicherry Lodge

Summary

At nearly 11pm, Holmes, Watson, Mary and Thaddeus Sholto arrive at Pondicherry Lodge. The door to the grounds is opened by McMurdo, who initially refuses entry to all but Thaddeus. However, when he recognises Holmes, he lets them in. (McMurdo is the first in a line of worthy 'good-guy' lower-class characters who like and respect Holmes.)

The garden is 'vast', the building is 'plunged in shadow' and 'its deathly silence struck a chill to the heart.' A cry is heard from Mrs Bernstone, the housekeeper, and Thaddeus enters. Meanwhile, Watson and Mary have a tender moment in the garden and hold hands. (The physical contact was quite risqué for the Victorian era so Watson includes the comment 'as she has often told me' to imply that they are actually married now.)

When they all enter the house, Mary comforts the housekeeper and the others go to Bartholomew's room. Holmes peers through the keyhole, followed by a 'sharp intaking of the breath'. He has seen only a face, illuminated by the moonlight – everything else is in darkness. Watson 'recoiled in horror' for the face looks exactly the same as Thaddeus'. It is his twin.

'The door must come down' instructs Holmes. They enter to find a gruesome body with a thorn in its neck, a club-like stick and a note with 'The sign of the four' upon it. Watson declares an 'insoluble mystery' but Holmes disagrees, 'On the contrary'. (Watson is often used as a foil to prompt Holmes to disagree with him, or to answer his questions and explain clues to the reader.)

Thaddeus enters and is horror-struck at his brother's death…and that the treasure has been taken. Thaddeus fears that he will be blamed for the crime but Holmes sends him to report the matter to the police, assuring him that he has 'no reason for fear'.

DO IT!

1 Re-read the scene between Holmes and McMurdo. How has Conan Doyle added some humour to the plot here? Quote McMurdo's **ironic** comment and explain how it is comic.

2 Re-read the final paragraph of the previous chapter from 'At the mention…' Find another comic moment here. (Note: strychnine is a powerful poison.)

 STRETCH IT!

Re-read the description of the body from 'By the table…'. Explore how Conan Doyle uses language to create a scene of horror. Pay particular attention to his use of strings of adjectives and explore the **connotations** of the details he has chosen.

Extract 1

There is great tension after the scream and Thaddeus enters the house. Watson, Mary and Holmes are in the darkened garden.

This scene is **framed**, as you might expect, with Holmes using his skills of observation. **1** Underline the language that shows how careful he is being.

In contrast to Holmes, Watson and Mary are focused on one another, rather than what is around them.

The scene is quite risqué for the Victorian era, with its strict rules about modesty and propriety.

Victorian belief in propriety meant that men, and women, should be above instinct (associated with animals). Again, Conan Doyle is pushing boundaries here. **2** Why would he do this?

" Our guide had left us the lantern. Holmes swung it slowly round, and peered keenly at the house, and at the great rubbish-heaps which cumbered the grounds. Miss Morstan and I stood together, and her hand was in mine. A wondrous subtle thing is love, for
5 here were we two who had never seen each other before that day, between whom no word or even look of affection had ever passed, and yet now in an hour of trouble our hands instinctively sought for each other. I have marvelled at it since, but at the time it seemed the most natural thing that I should go out to her so,
10 and, as she has often told me, there was in her also the instinct to turn to me for comfort and protection. So we stood hand in hand, like two children, and there was peace in our hearts for all the dark things that surrounded us. "

Conan Doyle makes the scene acceptable by implying that the relationship continued to honourable marriage. **3** What does Mary seek from Watson here? What does this suggest about gender roles at the time?

4 What does this analogy suggest about their behaviour and intentions?

AQA exam-style question

Starting with this extract, explore how Conan Doyle presents romance in the novel.

Write about:

- how Conan Doyle presents romance in this extract
- how Conan Doyle presents romance in the novel as a whole.

[30 marks]

DEFINE IT!

cumbered – cluttered

for – in the last sentence, it actually means 'despite'

modesty – behaviour considered suitable for women of the time

propriety – good behaviour that keeps within social conventions

Character and theme essentials

Using a Gothic fiction setting to increase tension

'**Gothic fiction**' refers to a **style** of writing that contains elements of fear, horror and gloom. Death often features. This genre tends to emphasise physical and metaphorical darkness – a darkened building can symbolise a dark soul within.

The description of Pondicherry Lodge closely follows a previous description of the evening, when conditions seem quite pleasant. Conan Doyle then chooses to describe the house itself in much gloomier and menacing terms:

Extract 1
Beginning of the chapter

> It was nearly eleven o'clock when we reached this final stage of our night's adventures. We had left the damp fog of the great city behind
> 5 us, and the night was fairly fine. A warm wind blew from the westward, and heavy clouds moved slowly across the sky, with half a moon peeping occasionally
> 10 through the rifts. It was clear enough to see for some distance, but Thaddeus Sholto took down one of the side-lamps from the carriage to give us a better light upon our way.

Extract 2
Before the group enter the house

> Inside, a gravel path wound through desolate grounds to a huge clump of a house, square and prosaic, all
> 5 plunged in shadow save where a moonbeam struck one corner and glimmered in a garret window. The vast size of the building, with its gloom
> 10 and its deathly silence, struck a chill to the heart. Even Thaddeus Sholto seemed ill at ease, and the lantern quivered and rattled in his hand.

Later, in true Gothic fashion, a body is discovered and described in full horrific detail.

Extract 3
The discovery of Bartholomew Sholto

> I stooped to the hole, and recoiled in horror. Moonlight was streaming into the room, and it was bright with a vague and shifty radiance. Looking straight at me, and
> 5 suspended, as it were, in the air, for all beneath was in shadow, there hung a face, – the very face of our companion Thaddeus. There was the same high, shining head, the same circular bristle of red hair, the same
> 10 bloodless countenance. The features were set, however, in a horrible smile, a fixed and unnatural grin, which in that still and moonlit room was more jarring to the nerves than any scowl or contortion.

REVIEW

IT!

1 Who answers the door to Pondicherry Lodge? How does he know Sherlock Holmes?

2 Holmes is told that he has 'wasted your gifts'. What is meant here? How might a reader react to this comment?

3 The previous chapter contained a long monologue by Thaddeus Sholto. This chapter mainly contains dialogue. Do you agree or disagree with the following statements about the novel's structure? For each statement, explain your choice.

a Conan Doyle needs a realistic perspective to deliver the background details of the treasure. Thaddeus provides that perspective.

b Dialogue allows character discovery alongside advance of the plot.

c Conan Doyle presents Holmes through dialogues as they best present his analytical stepped discoveries – a monologue would be too dense and less entertaining for a reader.

4 Who is Mrs Bernstone?

5 What noise do the whole group hear?

6 What does Mary do when she hears the noise?

7 Re-read the paragraph beginning 'Our guide had left us…' How is this paragraph very different to the novel so far?

8 Find two other examples from the novel so far focusing on a potential relationship between Mary and Watson. Does the sub-plot add to the novel? Explain your opinion.

9 Why has the garden been dug up?

10 When the group enter the house, what does Mary do? What reasons might Conan Doyle have for including this detail?

11 Who goes up to Brother Bartholomew's room?

12 On seeing Brother Bartholomew's body, the characters respond differently. Complete the table below.

Reaction	Name of the character	What it shows about the character
has a sharp intake of breath		
recoils in horror		
wrings his hands and moans in terror		

13 Find this section: '"The door must come down,"…Bartholomew Sholto's chamber.' Underline the phrases that create a sense of 'derring-do' and action. Why has Conan Doyle presented the characters in this way?

14 Find a quotation that makes the body appear gruesome. How might Bartholomew's appearance in death be explained? (Bear in mind Gothic conventions of ugliness/immorality and that Victorian readers compared appearances and morality.)

15 What is written on the note?

16 Name the other occasion on which this has been seen.

17 What has killed Bartholomew? How might this confirm a Victorian reader's view of things that are foreign to them?

18 How does Holmes behave with Thaddeus Sholto when Thaddeus sees his brother dead? Why has Conan Doyle presented Holmes in this way?

19 Has Mary been presented as a helpless female during this chapter? Explain your answer with reference to evidence from the text.

20 Until now, Holmes has been characterised as unemotional and intellectually superior. What new aspects of Holmes' character have been shown in this chapter?

Chapter Six

Sherlock Holmes Gives a Demonstration

Summary

Watson and Holmes search for evidence before the police return. Holmes notices a print made by a wooden leg. But, the wooden-legged man would not have been able to climb up without an ally. Holmes is excited by the unusual nature of the crime as it 'breaks fresh ground in the annals of crime in this country' – though he has known of similar cases in India and Senegambia. (Conan Doyle uses this comment to increase the excitement and exotic feel of the novel as well as illustrate the breadth of Holmes' knowledge.)

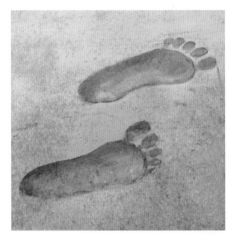

They explore the upper room where the treasure was found and find a small footprint. Holmes reacts with a 'startled, surprised look' but 'recovered his self-possession in an instant'. Watson felt that his 'skin was cold' as he thinks a child has made the print. Watson asks Holmes for his theory but is told to analyse the evidence for himself. (Notice that this is another of Conan Doyle's devices for delaying the disclosure of the culprit.)

Holmes uses a lens and tape measure to examine the prints and finds that the person had trodden in some creosote leaking from a tin. Holmes and Watson examine the body and find that the rigor mortis is unusual. The thorn in the neck that delivered the toxin is not from an English plant.

The police arrive, led by Athelney Jones, 'stout…red-faced' and with 'small twinkling eyes'. He is dismissive of Holmes' help in a previous case…but then asks him a question! Jones suspects Thaddeus stole the treasure; his opinion that 'His appearance is – well, not attractive' forms part of his evidence. Jones arrests Thaddeus. Holmes states his **interpretation** of events and refers to Jonathan Small. He promises to free Thaddeus and prove that Small is guilty. (This is the only time Small has been mentioned since Mary's note in Chapter Two. Neither the characters nor the reader know why Holmes thinks Small is responsible.)

Holmes refocuses on Mary's mystery. Watson comments that though he has seen 'something of the rough side of life', these events have 'shaken my nerve completely'. Holmes tells him to go to Sherman's to collect a dog, Toby, as he 'would rather have Toby's help than that of the whole detective force of London'.

The chapter ends with Holmes quoting Goethe, translated as: 'We are used to seeing that Man mocks what he never comprehends', referring to how Jones has treated him. (Holmes' intellect is shown by quoting philosophers, especially in other languages.)

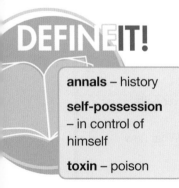

DEFINE IT!

annals – history

self-possession – in control of himself

toxin – poison

36

DO IT!

Extract 1

Thaddeus Sholto has been sent to get the police, giving Holmes some time to assess the crime scene.

Conan Doyle uses dialogues to show Holmes' reasoning processes.

Holmes' behaviour is in direct contrast to that of Athelney Jones, the policeman.
2 Find an example of Jones' overconfidence.

3 Are Holmes' questions **rhetorical**, or does he actually want Watson's opinion?

'Now, Watson,' said Holmes, rubbing his hands, 'we have half an hour to ourselves. Let us make good use of it. My case is, as I have told you, almost complete; but we must not err on the side of over-
5 confidence. Simple as the case seems now, there may be something deeper underlying it.'
'Simple!' I ejaculated.
'Surely,' said he, with something of the air of a clinical professor expounding to his class. 'Just sit
10 in the corner there, that your footprints may not complicate matters. Now to work! In the first place, how did these folk come, and how did they go? The door has not been opened since last night. How of the window?' He carried the lamp across
15 to it, muttering his observations aloud the while, but addressing them to himself rather than to me. 'Window is snibbed on the inner side. Framework is solid. No hinges at the side. Let us open it. No water-pipe near.
20 Roof quite out of reach. Yet a man has mounted by the window. It rained a little last night. Here is the print of a foot in mould upon the sill. And here is a circular muddy mark, and here again upon the floor, and here again by the table. See here,
25 Watson! This is really a very pretty demonstration.'

Conan Doyle often adds adverbials that function as 'stage directions' to enable the reader to easily visualise the scene. 1 What do you learn about Holmes from the adverbials used in this extract?

Watson's comments are used to emphasise Holmes' reactions.

Notice how Holmes' **sentence structures** change when he is focused on a task. 4 How does this differ from Holmes' language in Chapter One?

AQA exam-style question

Starting with this extract, explore how Conan Doyle presents Holmes in the novel.

Write about:

• how Conan Doyle presents Holmes in this extract

• how Conan Doyle presents Holmes in the novel as a whole.

[30 marks]

DEFINE IT!

ejaculated – here, it means spoken in a surprised tone

expounded – explained

pretty – here, it means enjoyable

snibbed – shut

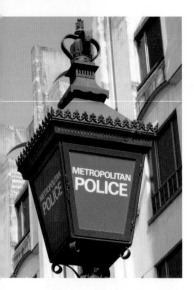

Character and theme essentials

The police and clues

The Metropolitan Police Force was established in 1829. Made up from working-class men, the early force was distrusted by the public, and focused mainly on preventing crime rather than detecting it. From 1842, crime detection became more prominent, and in 1877 the Criminal Investigation Department (CID) was created. Officers were still drawn from working-class men, not gentlemen like Holmes; Conan Doyle raises the Victorian distrust of the police and their effectiveness while Holmes also represents the superior intellect of 'gentlemen' over their social inferiors.

Conan Doyle was very interested in forensic techniques such as analysing fingerprints, footprints and chemical traces. However, these were not widely used by the police force of his time. In fact, the first conviction of a criminal using fingerprint evidence was not until 1902. Holmes embodies the scientist detective and is placed in contrast to the police force in this novel.

Athelney Jones and Sherlock Holmes

The police are criticised through the characterisation of Athelney Jones (lower-ranking police officers do not receive the same criticism). Jones noisily arrives at the crime scene, full of bluster:

> As he spoke, the steps which had been coming nearer sounded loudly on the passage, and a very stout, portly man in a grey suit strode heavily into the room. He was red-faced, burly and plethoric, with a pair of very small twinkling eyes which looked keenly out from between swollen and puffy pouches.

In contrast to Holmes' precision, Jones' detection techniques are found to be almost non-existent.

> 'Ha! I have a theory. These flashes come upon me at times…What do you think of this, Holmes? Sholto was, on his own confession, with his brother last night.
> 5 The brother died in a fit, on which Sholto walked off with the treasure. How's that?'

Holmes replies:

> On which the dead man very considerately got up and locked the door on the inside.

STRETCHIT!

What is Holmes' attitude towards Jones here and throughout the novel? Write a paragraph using examples to support your opinion.

DEFINEIT!

plethoric – excessive, in this case it suggests being overweight

DOIT!

Which of these adjectives can be applied to Athelney Jones? Support your choices with evidence from this chapter or the whole novel.

over-confident egotistical bumbling deferential critical unpleasant good-humoured
analytical careful bombastic comical talkative complimentary

REVIEW

IT!

1 What is the 'circular muddy mark'?

2 'Framework is solid. No hinges at the side. Let us open it.' What do you notice about Holmes' language here?

3 Compare the style of speech above with his language from Chapter One. Describe this variation in style.

4 Fill the gaps to complete Holmes' explanations.

The wooden-legged man entered through the _____. His ally entered through the _____. The wooden-legged man left _____ on the rope showing that he had _____ down it and _____ his hands.

5 Holmes refers to cases in India and Senegambia. What impression of Holmes is Conan Doyle giving to his readers?

6 When Holmes climbed up to the room above, 'seizing a rafter with either hand, he swung himself up into the garret'. What impression is given of Holmes here? Find another example of this side of his character.

7 Why does a 'surprised look' appear on Holmes' face? Give another occasion when he is presented like this. Why does Conan Doyle characterise Holmes in this way?

8 What makes Watson's skin go cold?

9 Watson compares Holmes to a bloodhound when he scans the room for clues. Name another animal Holmes is compared to in the novel. What is the connotation of these comparisons?

10 Who are the 'accredited representatives of the law'? Why does Holmes refer to them in this way?

11 The police are introduced with heavy steps, loud voices and a crash. Why has Conan Doyle introduced them in this way?

12 Choose one negative and one positive physical characteristic of Athelney Jones. Why has Conan Doyle presented him this way?

13 What does Athelney Jones call Holmes?

14 Describe Jones' attitude to Holmes.

15 Re-read the dialogue between Holmes and Jones. Find three descriptions of how Jones speaks to Holmes. What effect do they have on a reader?

16 Holmes deduces that Jonathan Small (circle one in each pair):

a is small   is tall

b is active   is unfit

c is pale   is sunburned

d has his left leg   has his right leg.

17 Who is Toby and what does Holmes want him to do?

18 List all the clues Holmes has observed in Bartholomew's room.

19 What have you learned about Holmes from his interaction with the police?

20 Do you have any sympathy for Thaddeus Sholto? Explain your response.

Chapter Seven: The Episode of the Barrel

Summary

On the journey to take Mary home, she is in a 'passion of weeping' with the strain of the evening's events. Watson is 'distant' as he is thinking that he cannot declare his affection at a moment like this, and because Mary will become his social superior. On arrival, Watson recaps events to her employer-friend, Mrs Forrester. (The novel was first serialised in a magazine; this recount allows a summary of the plot as a reminder for the first Victorian readers.)

Watson then collects Toby the dog. Watson is called a 'drunken vagabond' by Mr Sherman, but is then welcomed after saying that Holmes has sent him. (Add this to your collection of comic scenes that Conan Doyle uses to vary the levels of tension and deflation in the novel.)

On return to Pondicherry Lodge, Athelney Jones has been busy arresting everyone – including the housekeeper. Watson and Holmes re-examine the room where the treasure had been kept. Holmes pays particular attention to the footprint and then re-enacts the climb from the roof, finding a case containing poisoned thorn darts. (Again, Watson is used as a foil to prompt Holmes to deliver information in a **naturalistic** way.)

Toby sniffs a creosote-stained handkerchief and the chase begins. Watson asks Holmes how he knew about Jonathan Small and Holmes explains:

the letter from India must have been to tell Major Sholto that the convicts who had shared the map with him had escaped; the only English name was Small's; he must, therefore, be the wooden-legged man at the window at Major Sholto's death. He was 'mad with hate' at the Major's theft of his treasure. Small then waited until Bartholomew found the treasure, when he was informed by Bartholomew's Indian servant, Lal Rao. Because of Small's wooden leg, he would have needed help to scale the building, so he must have had an accomplice. Holmes believes that the ally, not Small, had murdered Bartholomew.

Holmes asks if Watson has his revolver to deal with Small (Watson only has his stick) as 'if the other turns nasty I shall shoot him dead'. (Tension has been intensified to this point and the reader expects the **climax** to follow.)

As they follow Toby, Watson notes 'the gleam in Holmes's eyes', which suggests the end is in sight. However, it turns out to be a false trail. Holmes and Watson 'burst simultaneously into an uncontrollable fit of laughter'.

Extract 1

Holmes and Watson are following Toby, the dog, who is tracking the scent of creosote from the footprints left at Pondicherry Lodge. They have arrived at a junction.

DEFINE IT!

creosote – a tar-based substance with a strong odour

deflation – here, the feelings of disappointment or excitement being reduced (instead of built-up)

tension – here, a reader's feelings of excitement

"

'What the deuce is the matter with the dog?' growled Holmes. 'They surely would not take a cab, or go off in a balloon.'

'Perhaps they stood here for some time,' I suggested.

'Ah! it's all right. He's off again,' said my companion, in a tone of relief.

5 He was indeed off, for after sniffing round again he suddenly made up his mind, and darted away with an energy and determination such as he had not yet shown. The scent appeared to be much hotter than before, for he had not even to put his nose on the ground, but tugged at his leash and tried to break into a run. I could see by the gleam in Holmes's eyes that he thought we were nearing the end of

10 our journey.

Our course now ran down Nine Elms until we came to Broderick and Nelson's large timber-yard, just past the White Eagle tavern. Here the dog, frantic with excitement, turned down through the side-gate into the enclosure, where the sawyers were already at work. On the dog raced through sawdust and shavings,

15 down an alley, round a passage, between two wood-piles, and finally, with a triumphant yelp, sprang upon a large barrel which still stood upon the hand-trolley on which it had been brought. With lolling tongue and blinking eyes, Toby stood upon the cask, looking from one to the other of us for some sign of appreciation. The staves of the barrel and the wheels of the trolley were smeared

20 with a dark liquid, and the whole air was heavy with the smell of creosote. Sherlock Holmes and I looked blankly at each other, and then burst simultaneously into an uncontrollable fit of laughter.

"

Conan Doyle is usually very **explicit** about how Holmes delivers his dialogue, but unusually he uses a metaphor here – coincidentally a dog is also involved in the plot at this point!

Conan Doyle often pairs his descriptions. It tends to give his style an air of precision – much like Holmes.

Watson often refers to the expression in Holmes' eyes, for example: 'languid', 'keen dark eyes'.

Notice how the author chooses a long sentence, full of adverbials telling which way Toby is going, to recreate the effect of the chase.

Holmes often reacts with humour – 'grinning', 'chuckling' – and, here, hilarity. This contrasts with the other side of Holmes' characterisation, when he is depicted as depressed, brooding or having dark moods.

DEFINE IT!

hand-trolley – a pull-along cart

Chapter Eight: The Baker Street Irregulars

Summary

Toby gets back on track. He takes them to a new location on the water's edge. (Conan Doyle includes a variety of locations in the novel – adding to the plot's dynamism.) It is apparent that Small and his accomplice have taken a boat from Mordecai Smith's boat rental.

Holmes engages a child and his mother in conversation. He encourages her to talk and she delivers information about her husband's disappearance on a mysterious trip with a wooden-legged man. Holmes shows his understanding of people, telling Watson that if people think the information you want is important, 'they will instantly shut up like an oyster'. (Holmes' interactions with the working classes are often humorous. Conan Doyle plays to his middle-class readers by stereotyping and recreating accents.)

Watson thinks their next course of action is clear – to follow them. Holmes disagrees. Watson then suggests calling the police or advertising for information as to their whereabouts. Holmes disagrees with both. (Yet again, Watson functions as a plot device to avoid Holmes continually explaining himself for no reason.)

Holmes sends a wire to the Baker Street division. We may assume that these are detectives, but later learn that they are a gang of children. It is now between 8 and 9am. Watson is 'befogged in mind and fatigued in body'. They return home and read a report in the newspaper of Athelney Jones' marvellous arrests, while Holmes is 'grinning over his coffee-cup'. (The report praises Jones' police work. Conan Doyle creates **irony** here, and Holmes enjoys the irony.)

Mrs Hudson then gives a 'wail of expostulation and dismay' as 'a dozen dirty and ragged little street-Arabs' enter: the Baker Street Irregulars. (Yet another group is introduced to the novel – this is a busy chapter for minor characters.) Holmes gives them instructions and they 'buzz' out again, 'streaming' down the street to find Small and his ally.

Holmes states his pleasure in the case: 'I never remember feeling tired by work, though idleness exhausts me completely.' Holmes gathers his evidence about Small's ally and then uses a gazetteer to look up information about potential savages. He identifies him as being an Andaman Island aborigine, known for violence and cannibalism.

To end the chapter, Holmes plays Watson to sleep with his violin. Watson dreams of 'the sweet face of Mary Morstan looking down upon me'.

DEFINE IT!

dynamism – energy and activity

gazetteer – a book containing information about the geographical, social and physical features of a country

stereotyping – presenting a type of person rather than an individual

wire – telegram

Extract 1

Holmes engages the wife and child of the boatman Mordecai Smith in conversation, to find out what he needs to know. Conan Doyle includes several dialogues with lower-class characters, using accents. Why might a reader enjoy these dialogues?

> <u>'A fine child, Mrs Smith!'</u>
>
> 'Lor' bless you, sir, he is that, and forward. He gets a'most too much for me to manage, 'specially when my man is away days at a time.'
>
> <u>'Away, is he?'</u> said Holmes, in a disappointed voice. 'I am sorry for that, for I
> 5 wanted to speak to Mr Smith.'
>
> 'He's been away since yesterday mornin', sir, and, truth to tell, I am beginnin' to feel frightened about him. But if it was about a boat, sir, maybe I could serve as well.'
>
> 'I wanted to hire his steam launch.'
>
> 'Why, bless you, sir, it is in the steam launch that he has gone. That's what puzzles
> 10 me; for I know there ain't more coals in her than would take her to about Woolwich and back. If he'd been away in the barge I'd ha' thought nothin'; for many a time a job has taken him as far as Gravesend, and then if there was much doin' there he might ha' stayed over. But what good is a steam launch without coals?'
>
> 'He might have bought some at a wharf down the river.'
>
> 15 'He might, sir, but it weren't his way. Many a time I've heard him call out at the prices they charge for a few odd bags. Besides, I don't like that wooden-legged man, wi' his ugly face and outlandish talk. What did he want always knockin' about here for?'
>
> 'A wooden-legged man?' said Holmes, with bland surprise.
>
> 20 'Yes, sir, a brown, monkey-faced chap that's called more'n once for my old man…I tell you straight, sir, I don't feel easy in my mind about it.'

To create Mrs Smith's voice, Conan Doyle uses:

- abbreviation
- **colloquial language**
- rhetorical questions.

As noted before, Conan Doyle gives precise directions as to how Holmes should speak. Here, they are added using adverbials.

References to Jonathan Small reinforce his unpleasant appearance, suggestive of the wickedness within. However, when Holmes actually meets him, he is presented in a much more human way.

1 How can you tell that Mrs Smith is of a lower class than Holmes?

2 Holmes encourages Mrs Smith to open up to him. Two examples are underlined in the extract above. Find three further examples. What does this show you about Holmes? Explain your opinion.

AQA exam-style question

Starting with this extract, explore how Conan Doyle presents working-class characters in the novel. Write about:

- how Conan Doyle presents working-class characters here
- how Conan Doyle presents working-class characters in the novel as a whole.

[30 marks]

Character and theme essentials

> Through his work as a doctor and service on ships, Conan Doyle would have had contact with a wide range of people and presents working classes with dignity.

Holmes and the working classes

There are several interactions between Holmes and working-class characters in the novel:

- McMurdo, the prizefighter
- Mrs Smith, the boatman's wife
- Wiggins and the Baker Street Irregulars
- Jonathan Small.

Conan Doyle introduces humour in each of the exchanges, entertaining his readers. Victorian divisions between classes were highly defined. Each class would have found humour in the differences and behaviours of another class. Comedians, TV shows and writers do this today by making jokes about particular groups within society – the best do so without causing offence.

Conan Doyle invites his middle-class readers to smile at the working classes through Watson's narration – they are likely to share his perspective – but he does not criticise them in this novel. Holmes treats these characters with respect and appears to like them. They are all helpful to Holmes, which gains the reader's approval. Ironically, Holmes' universal appeal to all the characters he meets – including those considered disreputable by his middle-class readership – adds to his status as a gentleman, respected by all.

Wiggins

Holmes uses colloquial language to refer to Wiggins, the Baker Street Irregular – 'my dirty little lieutenant' – which implies a fondness rather than a criticism. The children are 'street-Arabs', meaning that they are homeless urchins who survive by begging and stealing.

In Chapter Ten, Holmes refers to the 'Dirty-looking rascals' (the working-class people on the waterfront) having an 'immortal spark' within them. This similarity of language implies that Holmes is fond of lower-class humanity.

DO IT!

Using the extract below, explain how Holmes uses the situation to his advantage.
The following questions will help you to plan your answer:

- How does Holmes treat the boy Jack? Underline your evidence.

- Why does he treat the boy in this way?

- Which social class does the boy belong to? Why does Conan Doyle give Holmes the upper hand in this scene?

STRETCH IT!

Explain how Conan Doyle entertains the reader with humour in this scene.

> 'Dear little chap!' said Holmes, strategically. 'What a rosy-cheeked young rascal! Now, Jack, is there anything you would like?'
> The youth pondered for a moment. 'I'd like a shillin',' said he.
> 'Nothing you would like better?'
> 5 'I'd like two shillin' better,' the prodigy answered, after some thought.

REVIEW IT!

Chapter Seven: Episode of the Barrel

1 How does Mary change when she is in the cab?

2 Why does Watson say, 'Worse still, she was rich'?

3 Mr Sherman calls Watson a 'drunken vagabond'. Why has Conan Doyle included this scene? Which other events are similar to this one?

4 Who has Athelney Jones arrested? What is Conan Doyle's intended reader response to this news?

5 We see Holmes climb down from the roof. Why does he do this? What does he find? How does the reader respond to Holmes in this scene?

6 Find two things that Holmes deduces about Jonathan Small.

7 Why does Holmes ask Watson if he has a pistol? What effect does the mention of weapons have on the reader?

8 Toby makes a mistake. What is the mistake and why has it happened?

9 What does Watson notice about Holmes' eyes as they near the end of the pursuit?

10 What do Watson and Holmes do at the end of this chapter? Compare this moment to their characterisation in Chapter One. Briefly summarise how their characters have developed.

Chapter Eight: Baker Street Irregulars

1 Which location does this chapter open with? List other locations from the novel. Why does Conan Doyle name so many parts of London?

2 How did Holmes manage to open a conversation with Mrs Smith?

3 Watson is used again as a foil to allow Holmes to show how superior his mind is. How many times does Watson offer an incorrect solution?

4 Re-read the news report. Find two examples of irony (something happening in a way contrary to what is expected, causing some amusement) that Conan Doyle uses to mock the police in this report.

5 Who are the Baker Street Irregulars?

6 What is implied about Holmes' character from the fact that he knows this group?

7 'A savage!' What was the Victorian attitude to people from more remote countries?

8 What does the 'gazetteer' say about the Andaman Island aborigines? What might be the effect on a Victorian reader? How might a modern reader respond?

9 Which new talent of Holmes is introduced in this chapter?

10 Look at the endings of the previous two chapters and this one. What do you notice about how Conan Doyle ends some of the chapters? Why does he do this?

Chapter Nine

A Break in the Chain

Summary

It is late in the afternoon when Watson wakes to find Holmes 'dark and troubled' because he appears not to have a lead in the case at this time. Watson leaves to return Toby and to call at Mary's home. Holmes advises him that 'Women are never to be entirely trusted'. (Conan Doyle allows Holmes to be controversial. Imagine the reaction to this from his female readers! Would they laugh it off – as we do with some controversial comedians – or would they be offended?)

Mrs Forrester describes the night's events as 'a romance': dragons, knights, and evil **antagonists**. Mary gives a 'bright glance' at Watson. She is concerned for Thaddeus Sholto but not about the inheritance.

Watson returns to find Mrs Hudson concerned about Holmes' lack of sleep; he looks 'worn and haggard'. He leaves to visit Mary again, returning in the evening. Holmes is conducting a 'malodorous experiment'. At dawn, Watson is awoken by Holmes dressed as a sailor and going off to make enquiries on the river. Watson remains at the apartment and reads a newspaper report of the case giving credit to Athelney Jones, but also stating that Thaddeus Sholto and his housekeeper have been released.

Watson considers whether Holmes could be mistaken, misled by 'some radical flaw'. But, after thinking it through, he decides 'I had never known him to be wrong'.

Athelney Jones arrives 'downcast…meek and even apologetic', as Holmes sent him a note asking him to call. (Conan Doyle could have stereotyped the policeman completely, but he chooses to show a more agreeable side to his character.) Watson is hospitable and they wait for Holmes.

An aged sailor arrives. He refuses to give information to Watson, insisting that he will only speak to Holmes. In fact, the sailor is Holmes.

Holmes has a plan and tells Jones 'you must act on the line that I point out', but is happy for Jones to take the credit for any success. He requires a fast police-boat and two strong men, and he requests that Watson is able to deliver the treasure to Mary and that Holmes can interview Jonathan Small when he is caught. Jones agrees and Holmes invites him to dine with them.

DO IT!

Mrs Forrester refers to Watson's account of the night's events as a 'romance'. Use the prompts below to help you consider how far the whole novel might be considered a 'romance':

- Who are the protagonists and antagonists in the novel?

- To what extent is there a battle of good versus evil?

- Does good prevail?

Extract 1

Holmes has sent a wire (a telegram) to Athelney Jones, asking him to meet at Baker Street.

> 'How has your case prospered?'
>
> 'It has all come to nothing. I have had to release two of my prisoners, and there is no evidence against the other two.'
>
> 'Never mind. We shall give you two others in the place of them. But you must put
> 5 yourself under my orders. You are welcome to all the official credit, but you must act on the line that I point out. Is that agreed?'
>
> 'Entirely, if you will help me to the men.'
>
> 'Well, then, in the first place I shall want a fast police-boat – a steam launch – to be at the Westminster Stairs at seven o'clock.'
>
> 10 'That is easily managed. There is always one about there; but I can step across the road and telephone to make sure.'
>
> 'Then I shall want two staunch men, in case of resistance.'
>
> 'There will be two or three in the boat. What else?'
>
> 'When we secure the men we shall get the treasure. I think that it would be a
> 15 pleasure to my friend here to take the box round to the young lady to whom half of it rightfully belongs. Let her be the first to open it. – Eh, Watson?'
>
> 'It would be a great pleasure to me.'
>
> 'Rather an irregular proceeding,' said Jones, shaking his head. 'However, the whole thing is irregular, and I suppose we must wink at it. The treasure must
> 20 afterwards be handed over to the authorities until after the official investigation.'
>
> 'Certainly. That is easily managed. One other point. I should much like to have a few details about this matter from the lips of Jonathan Small himself. You know I like to work the detail of my cases out. There is no objection to my having an unofficial interview with him, either here in my rooms or elsewhere, as long as he
> 25 is efficiently guarded?'

Notice how the sense of failure is magnified here through the juxtaposition of positive and negative vocabulary.

Holmes uses the language of obligation. Is this arrogance or necessary instruction? Can you find other examples of this manner of speech?

Jones could have just said that he would arrange the boat, so why has Conan Doyle chosen to include this detail?

DOIT!

Look at the green highlight. Why does Holmes make this request? What does it show about his relationship with Watson?

 STRETCHIT!

1 Look at the purple highlight. Is Jones using colloquial or formal language here? Is Jones the same social class as Holmes?

2 Look at the grey highlight. Is Holmes making a statement or a request at this point? Is this a different tone of voice for Holmes? Why might he use this tone here?

 AQA exam-style question

Starting with this extract, explore how Conan Doyle presents Holmes' relationship with the police in the novel.

Write about:

- how Conan Doyle presents Holmes' relationship with the police in this extract
- how Conan Doyle presents Holmes' relationship with the police in the novel as a whole.

[30 marks]

Theme and character essentials

Structural variety

Conan Doyle extends the reader's entertainment through the novel's clever structure. Overall, the novel has a **linear narrative** and a tight **chronology** – events happen across a short space of time. However, this chapter serves almost as a **hiatus** (pause) – organising events before the main climax of action occurs. (Although tension is probably the most entertaining element for a reader of detective fiction, non-stop tension would be dull. Conan Doyle varies his narrative so that the reader is moved through different levels of intensity. Think about why he does this.)

Plot and sub-plot

The detection plot is varied with moments when the romantic sub-plot is placed in primary focus, or, as in this case, when the romantic sub-plot is used to remind the reader of details from previous chapters.

1 Because the novel was serialised, Conan Doyle needs to frequently remind his readers of elements of the plot. What is he reminding us about at each of the highlighted points in this extract?

> 'Why, Mary, your fortune depends upon the issue of this search. I don't think that you are nearly excited enough. Just imagine what it must be to be so rich, and to have the world at your feet!'
> It sent a little thrill of joy to my heart to notice that she showed no sign of elation at the
> 5 prospect. On the contrary, she gave a toss of her proud head, as though the matter were one in which she took small interest.
> 'It is for Mr Thaddeus Sholto that I am anxious,' she said. 'Nothing else is of any consequence; but I think that he has behaved most kindly and honourably throughout. It is our duty to clear him of this dreadful and unfounded charge.'

2 a Give each event from Chapter Nine a score (0–5) for how exciting it is.

- Holmes is 'dark and troubled'. ☐
- Mrs Hudson is worried about Holmes' health. ☐
- Watson goes to visit Mary. ☐
- Holmes leaves the house. ☐
- Watson reads the newspaper. ☐
- Jones visits Baker Street. ☐
- Holmes tricks Watson and Jones with his disguise. ☐
- Arrangements are made to collaborate on the capture. ☐

b What do you notice about the level of excitement in this chapter? Why do you think Conan Doyle has written a whole chapter in which the case does not progress very much?

REVIEW

IT!

1 What makes Holmes appear 'dark and troubled'?

2 'Women are never to be entirely trusted – not the best of them.' Suggest two reasons why Conan Doyle may have included this opinion.

3 What does Mrs Forrester mean by 'a romance'?

4 Describe Mary's attitude to the potential inheritance. Why does Conan Doyle include this?

5 Mrs Hudson and Watson are both worried about Holmes. Why? How does this affect the readers' view of Holmes?

6 Why do you think it is important that Holmes is a fallible hero (one who can be mistaken)?

7 What does Holmes spend the evening in his room doing?

8 What does Holmes dress himself as? Why does he do this? Where is he going?

9 Name the two items that Watson sees in the newspaper.

10 'Was it not possible that his nimble and speculative mind had built up this wild theory upon faulty premises?' What is Watson concerned about here?

11 Watson doubts Holmes but comes to a conclusion. Find and quote the sentence that sums up Watson's belief in Holmes from the paragraph beginning 'This was clearly Holmes's doing'.

12 Who arrives at 3pm? Why has he come?

13 How is Jones' attitude different from the last time they met?

14 Why does Jones agree to have a whiskey and soda? What might be a reader's reaction to this?

15 How has Conan Doyle presented the police in the novel so far?

16 Jones says, 'I think he would have made a most promising officer.' On what other occasion is Holmes told that he could have had a different career?

17 Holmes returns disguised as an aged sailor. How does Conan Doyle introduce humour to this scene?

18 Holmes is to be 'master of the situation' to track down the treasure. Fill the gaps to show what he requires: a fast _____, _____ strong men, Watson to deliver the _____, to talk to _____.

19 Holmes invites Jones to supper. What does this indicate about Holmes?

20 Notice how this chapter functions as preparation for the climax of the case rather than significantly advancing the events of the plot. Thus, it has a rather fragmentary structure. Number the 'fragments' to put them in the correct order. The first has been done for you.

Arrangements are made for seizing the treasure. ☐

Holmes disguises himself. ☐

Watson visits Mary and returns Toby. ☐

Watson is concerned about Holmes. 1

Watson converses with Jones. ☐

Holmes carries out some experiments. ☐

49

Chapter Ten: The End of the Islander

Summary

Watson observes that Jones is 'a sociable soul in his hours of relaxation' and that Holmes 'could talk exceedingly well when he chose' while they have supper. At about 6.30pm, taking revolvers, they leave to meet a fast police boat at Westminster Wharf, whence Holmes has traced the *Aurora,* ready for Small's escape.

Holmes had checked all the repair yards until he found her. He had put himself 'in the place of Small' to anticipate his moves (because Small has 'a certain degree of low cunning' and is capable of 'delicate finesse' in his planning). The *Aurora* has been hidden but is ready for a getaway. On hearing this, Jones and Watson recommend solutions: Holmes explains why both ideas would fail. (Conan Doyle uses dialogue to demonstrate Holmes' superiority over Watson and Jones.) A Baker Street Irregular stands sentry by the boat-yard, to signal when the *Aurora* begins to leave.

A flag is waved. The police boat 'roared…whizzed…clanked' and they close on the speeding *Aurora*. Then, a barge pulls out in front of them and they lose ground. Watson enjoys the 'wild thrill' of the chase and Holmes urges to go greater speed. Gaining ground again, they see Small and a 'dark mass'. With Small shouting at the police boat, the Islander stands up – a 'savage, distorted creature…deeply marked with all bestiality and cruelty'. The Islander prepares a dart but Holmes and Watson shoot. The Islander falls overboard. Watson sees his 'menacing eyes amid the white swirl of the waters'. Small turns the boat for land. He jumps out to escape…but finds himself stuck in the mud. He then has to be hauled out with a rope 'like some evil fish'. (Notice how Conan Doyle escalates tension and then deflates it with a moment of humour.)

Holmes notices a dart in the wood of the boat; it had passed between himself and Watson. Watson is 'turned…sick' by thoughts of a horrible death. Holmes merely 'shrugged his shoulders in his easy fashion'.

DEFINE IT!

bestiality – behaviour like an animal's

low cunning – basic trickery

Conan Doyle presents Jonathan Small in several different ways throughout the novel.
Complete the table to summarise the change that occurs in this chapter.
Why has Conan Doyle altered his presentation of Small's character at this point in the novel?

		What is implied about Small?
Chapter Four	'a bearded, hairy face, with wild cruel eyes and an expression of concentrated malevolence'	
Chapter Ten	He is said to have 'delicate finesse… That is usually a product of higher education.' 'This man Small is a pretty shrewd fellow.'	

Extract 1

On board the police boat, Holmes, Watson and Jones are in pursuit of Jonathan Small and the Islander, Tonga.

> Here, as is usual, Holmes' speech is described in greater detail than that of other characters. The verb choices are succinct so as not to interrupt the chase sequence.

'And there is the *Aurora*,' exclaimed Holmes, 'and going like the devil! Full speed ahead, engineer. Make after that launch with the yellow light. By heaven, I shall never forgive myself if she proves to have the heels of us!'

She had slipped unseen through the yard-entrance and passed behind two or
5 three small craft, so that she had fairly got her speed up before we saw her. Now she was flying down the stream, near in to the shore, going at a tremendous rate. Jones looked gravely at her and shook his head.

'She is very fast,' he said. 'I doubt if we shall catch her.'

'We *must* catch her!' cried Holmes, between his teeth. 'Heap it on, stokers!
10 Make her do all she can! If we burn the boat we must have them!'

We were fairly after her now. The furnaces roared, and the powerful engines whizzed and clanked, like a great metallic heart. Her sharp, steep prow cut through the river-water and sent two rolling waves to right and to left of us. With every throb of the engines we sprang and quivered like a living thing. One great
15 yellow lantern in our bows threw a long, flickering funnel of light in front of us. Right ahead a dark blur upon the water showed where the *Aurora* lay, and the swirl of white foam behind her spoke of the pace at which she was going. We flashed past barges, steamers, merchant-vessels, in and out, behind this one and round the other. Voices hailed us out of the darkness, but still the *Aurora*
20 thundered on, and still we followed close upon her track.

 **DO IT!**

1 How is Holmes' speech here used to increase tension for the reader?
Underline phrases that:
- increase pace
- increase urgency
- imply possible failure.

2 Look at the blue highlight. Conan Doyle creates a soundscape to help build the tension of this chase. Find three more words that add to this effect.

3 Look at the pink highlight. Conan Doyle doesn't use a lot of metaphor, so the reader tends to notice when he does so. What does this **simile** imply about the boat and how does it add to the tension of the chase?

4 Look at the green highlight. Similar to the last chase sequence with Toby, Conan Doyle uses sentence structure to suggest a sense of speed. Explain how this is achieved here.

AQA exam-style question

Starting with this extract, explore how Conan Doyle creates tension in the novel.

Write about:
- how Conan Doyle creates tension in this extract
- how Conan Doyle creates tension in the novel as a whole.

[30 marks]

Chapter Eleven: The Great Agra Treasure

Summary

Small is 'reckless-eyed', and 'a man who was not to be easily turned from his purpose'. Watson even notes a 'gleam of something like humour' in his 'twinkling eyes'. (Conan Doyle is careful to make Small seem very human after stereotyping him as a criminal in previous chapters.)

Holmes offers to prove that Small did not kill Bartholomew Sholto. Small describes how the Agra treasure is cursed: his first contact, Achmet, was murdered for it; Major Sholto suffered fear and guilt; Small has spent his time in 'slavery' due to the treasure. (Mention of a curse adds further exoticism and romance to the treasure, as the reader will wonder whether it may curse Mary.)

Athelney Jones is his more pompous self, implying that he played a major part in solving the mystery. Holmes gives a 'slight smile' at this. (Conan Doyle showed Jones favourably in the last chapter but is renewing his ironic perspective on the policeman.)

Watson takes the treasure to Mary's house. When she sees him, 'a bright flush of surprise…coloured her pale cheeks'. She listens to the night's events with 'shining eyes' and 'turned so white' that Watson thought she might faint. (Mary is portrayed as weaker at the end of the novel than she appeared at the start.)

Watson breaks the lock on the box and Mary opens it. There is no treasure. 'Thank God!', they both say. Watson can now declare his love as Mary is not wealthy (and therefore not out of his reach). They embrace and Watson ends with 'Whoever had lost a treasure, I knew that night that I had gained one.'

DOIT!

Various threads of the plot come to a conclusion in this chapter. How far are you satisfied with these **resolutions**? Explain your reasoning. An example has been done for you.

Plot resolution	Satisfied? Yes/No	Why do you feel this way?
The treasure box is opened.	Yes	I enjoyed the suspense of opening the box – it has a fairy-tale aspect to it that is suggestive of the balance between good and evil in the novel. I also enjoy the irony that the treasure has gone, which is a fitting end – wealth has only brought tragedy – and fits with the moral of the narrative.
Small is captured.		
Watson and Mary declare their love.		
Holmes resolves the case.		

Extract 1

Watson is taking the treasure box to Mary's home to open it with her. As he arrives, he sees her from the roadside. This scene in the novel is more typical of the kind of 'romantic fiction' (a love story) we might read today.

> She was seated by the open window, dressed in some sort of white diaphanous material, with a little touch of scarlet at the neck and waist. The soft light of a shaded lamp fell upon her as she leaned back in the basket chair, playing over her sweet, grave face, and tinting with a dull, metallic sparkle the rich coils of her
> 5 luxuriant hair. One white arm and hand drooped over the side of the chair, and her whole pose and figure spoke of an absorbing melancholy. At the sound of my footfall she sprang to her feet, however, and a bright flush of surprise and of pleasure coloured her pale cheeks.
> 'I heard a cab drive up,' she said. 'I thought that Mrs Forrester had come back very
> 10 early, but I never dreamed that it might be you. What news have you brought me?'
> 'I have brought something better than news,' said I, putting down the box upon the table and speaking jovially and boisterously, though my heart was heavy within me. 'I have brought you something which is worth all the news in the world. I have brought you a fortune.'

Aristocratic status was dependent upon birth and ownership of land. Middle-class status was dependent upon background and, very importantly, upon finances. Mary could move from a lowly position within this class (as an employee of Mrs Forrester) to financial independence. This would have been seen as a desirable outcome to a Victorian readership. Her pleasure at the loss of the fortune is idealistic rather than realistic, but it emphasises the 'treasure' that she finds in her love for Watson.

AQA exam-style question

Starting with this extract, explore how Conan Doyle presents Watson in the novel.

Write about:

- how Conan Doyle presents Watson in this extract
- how Conan Doyle presents Watson in the novel as a whole.

[30 marks]

 STRETCHIT!

Watson brings Mary the treasure. Explain the irony that Mary is also Watson's 'treasure'.

Conan Doyle presents the reader with a typical scene from romantic fiction.

Match these features with the quotations highlighted in the passage:

- description of beauty
- dimmed lighting
- an air of sadness
- increased heart-rate
- moments of uncertainty
- sense of expectation.

Remind yourself of the description of Mary's outfit in Chapter Two. How is this dress similar? Why does Conan Doyle present Mary in this way?

Character and theme essentials

Context: Racism

In the Victorian era it was acceptable to hold what we would now call a racist **viewpoint**. The average Victorian middle-class reader would know of other countries, but would know little about those further than France. The Empire was growing (see page 72). Products from far-flung countries were arriving in Britain, but migration was very limited. The Victorian reader was likely to have thought of foreigners as different from themselves, dangerous and probably dirty.

Tonga the Islander

Up to and including this chapter, Tonga the Islander, is presented as 'non-human' – he is only referred to by name by Jonathan Small in the subsequent chapters. Watson represents the middle-class reader's perspective and presents the Islander as 'savage' and fearsome.

> At the sound of his strident, angry cries there was movement in the huddled bundle upon the deck. It straightened itself into a little black man – the smallest I have ever seen – with a great, misshapen
> 5 head and a shock of tangled, dishevelled hair. Holmes had already drawn his revolver, and I whipped out mine at the sight of this savage, distorted creature. He was wrapped in some sort of dark ulster or blanket, which left only his face
> 10 exposed; but that face was enough to give a man a sleepless night. Never have I seen features so deeply marked with all bestiality and cruelty. His small eyes glowed and burned with a sombre light, and his thick lips were writhed back from his teeth, which grinned
> 15 and chattered at us with a half animal fury.

Each novel is a product of its time. Thus, racism is part of this novel. How might a modern reader respond to this presentation of the Islander?

DO IT!

1 Identify all the negative **imagery** used to present the Islander. Explain what you learn about Victorians from Watson's presentation of him.

2 'Somewhere in the dark ooze at the bottom of the Thames lie the bones of that strange visitor to our shores.'

Does Conan Doyle create any sympathy for the death of the Islander in these last words?

Treasure and greed

References to 'treasure' feature both literally and metaphorically in *The Sign of Four*.

The basis of the plot is a quest to find the origin of mysterious treasures: firstly, the pearls; then, the greater horde of treasure; next, the history of the treasure. Along the way, the treasure is actually hidden again by Jonathan Small throwing it into the River Thames. As Mrs Forrester says, the tale is a 'romance', having a fairy-tale quality because of the presence of treasure. So, while Conan Doyle includes great precision in terms of tracing evidence and setting locations, the novel retains an 'unreal' atmosphere because of our connotations of 'treasure' from myth and fairy tale.

In the next chapter, however, Small recounts the history of the treasure and it is more easily seen as 'loot' – something stolen in a time of war. Despite the description of the treasure's wealth and beauty, it is tarnished by the all too real bloodshed of the Indian Mutiny of 1857, and it is the men's greed that is foregrounded rather than the treasure itself.

Metaphorically, Watson and Mary find the 'treasure' of love. Watson ends this chapter with:

> Whoever had lost a treasure, I knew that night that I had gained one.

Ironically, the Agra treasure had been a hindrance for Watson:

> 'The treasure is lost,' said Miss Morstan, calmly.
> As I listened to the words and realized what they meant, a great shadow seemed to pass from my soul… It was selfish, no doubt, disloyal, wrong, but I could realize nothing save that the golden barrier was gone from between us.

DO IT!

Explain why Watson used the metaphor of a 'golden barrier'.

STRETCH IT!

To what extent are characters rewarded for 'moral' behaviour in the novel?

Read this answer to this question. Do you agree with the writer? Explain your opinion.

Conan Doyle does seem to hold a moral perspective through his presentation of the theme of treasure in this novel. Mary seeks the treasure out of curiosity for her past and the possible discovery of what happened to her father; she is content with her lot in life. Throughout the novel, she increases her happiness through her relationship with Watson. She is rewarded for her absence of greed. Watson, too, is rewarded for his generosity of spirit by attaining Mary's affections. He is alarmed by her potential fortune rather than seeking it as a 'fortune-hunter'. Greedy characters are punished - Major Sholto, Captain Morstan, Small and the other characters locked in the Indian gaol all suffer physical consequences for their greed.

REVIEW IT!

Chapter Ten: The End of the Islander

1 What do we learn about Holmes at the start of this chapter?

2 What do we learn about Athelney Jones at the start of this chapter?

3 Conan Doyle focuses on the speed of the police boat – it 'shot past' and 'overhauled' other boats. Why does he do this?

4 Holmes summarises Jonathan Small's plans for Watson. Fill in the gaps to complete the summary. Small wants to escape to _____ so he has a boat ready to take him to the _____. He has hidden the boat in a _____ where it will not be seen.

5 Holmes seems to admire Small a little. Why might he admire him?

6 How would Jones have attempted to capture Small?

7 How would Watson have attempted to capture Small?

8 While they await a signal from the Baker Street boy, what do Holmes and Watson talk about? Why does Conan Doyle present them like this?

9 Read the paragraph beginning 'We were fairly after her now…' Find three ways that tension is created by the language of this paragraph.

10 How do Holmes' words to the stokers, 'Pile it on, men, pile it on', increase the tension?

11 'Beside him lay a dark mass which looked like a Newfoundland dog.' Why does Conan Doyle avoid saying that this is the Islander?

12 Watson refers to his past, 'I have coursed many creatures in many countries…' When has he referred to his past before? Why does Conan Doyle choose for Watson to make these comparisons?

13 Watson describes the savage with great intensity. What is the intended effect on the reader?

14 What is the last moment the Islander is seen? Find the quotation and comment on the intended effect on the reader.

15

> " It was a wild and desolate place, where the moon glimmered upon a wide expanse of marsh-land, with pools of stagnant water and beds of decaying vegetation. "

Using your understanding of pathetic fallacy and Gothic conventions from pages 26 and 34, explore why Conan Doyle ended the chase here.

16

> " Somewhere in the dark ooze at the bottom of the Thames lie the bones of that strange visitor to our shores. "

What effect does Conan Doyle want with this ending of the chase?

17 Holmes discovers a dart. How do his and Watson's reactions differ?

18 Identify three ways in which tension is created in this chapter.

19 Holmes began the novel portrayed as an intellectual. What aspect of his character is developed in this chapter?

20 Conan Doyle wrote this novel to entertain his readers. Do you find this chapter entertaining? Why?

Chapter Eleven: The Great Agra Treasure

1 Select three details from the opening description that show Jonathan Small as having positive characteristics.

2 Why do you think Conan Doyle has avoided stereotype in his presentation of Small?

3 How does Holmes' attitude to Small reflect Holmes' social conscience?

4 The Islander, Tonga, is presented as evil. Give two examples of how Small refers to him. Why has Conan Doyle presented him in this way?

5 Holmes refers to Tonga as 'this black fellow'. Is Holmes racist?

6 Why would Small have been happy to have killed Major Sholto but not Bartholomew?

7 Why had Tonga left his dart and stick? Why is Conan Doyle telling us this?

8 What makes Small show a 'bitter smile'? Is this ironic? Give your opinion.

9 Fill the gaps with a word or phase.

The 'curse' of the treasure brought _____ to Achmet, _____ to Major Sholto and _____ to Small.

10 How does Conan Doyle delay opening the box?

11 Jones arrives and immediately asks for 'a pull at that flask, Holmes'. What does he want? Why has Conan Doyle included this detail?

12 How does Jones make a 'slight smile' appear on Holmes' face?

13 Where is Mary seated when Watson arrives? Why has Conan Doyle placed her there?

14 Give two examples of how Watson describes Mary. Is he a neutral **narrator**? What do your examples imply about Watson's feelings towards Mary?

15 Why is Watson's heart 'heavy within' him?

16 When hearing of the evening's events, Mary 'turned so white' that Watson thought she might faint. Has Mary become a stereotype?

17 How does Conan Doyle create tension in this scene?

> **❝**
>
> There was in the front a thick and broad hasp, wrought in the image of a sitting Buddha. Under this I thrust the end of the poker and twisted it outward as a lever. The hasp sprang open with a loud snap. With trembling fingers I flung back the lid. We both stood gazing in astonishment. The box was empty!
>
> **❞**

18 What does Watson mean by 'the golden barrier was gone from between us'?

19 Watson declares his love. How might a Victorian reader respond? How might a modern reader respond?

20 Most threads of the narrative are resolved in this chapter, but Conan Doyle still leaves curiosity in the reader's mind. Which questions remain unresolved?

Chapter Twelve

The Strange Story of Jonathan Small

Summary

Watson returns to Baker Street. Jonathan Small 'laughed aloud' because he had thrown the treasure in the River Thames, saying if 'the three men who are in the Andaman convict barracks' can't have it, no one shall. Athelney Jones refers to 'justice' and Small shows his anger in 'a wild whirl of words'. He recounts his life story and the story of the Agra treasure.

Flashback

Small comes from a respectable lower-class background. He joins the army to avoid trouble at home. While serving in India, a crocodile bites off part of his leg and he is invalided out of the army. He works for a planter (farmer) on the recommendation of the colonel.

The Indian Mutiny of 1857 breaks out. There is bloodshed and chaos, 'the black fiends…dancing and howling'. Small heads for the British fort at Agra, 'swarming with fanatics and fierce devil-worshippers'. Small is on guard duty, along with Abdullah Khan and Mahomet Singh. They rebel and offer him the choice to die or steal the treasure with them and Dost Akbar (escort to Achmet, servant of a rajah). Small has only a moment to think: life is a 'sacred thing' but not when there is 'fire and blood all around you' – being in a war zone changes the perspective. (Conan Doyle inserts Watson's perspective to remind the reader of the context of this: Watson describes his own 'utmost horror' and Holmes' 'disgust' at Small's cold manner of describing these horrific events.) They kill Achmet and take the treasure.

The four men swear and sign an oath after hiding the body and the treasure. However, Achmet was being followed, is reported missing and a search is carried out. The four are all imprisoned. Small 'bided my time', knowing that he had treasure hidden away. Transferred to the Andaman Islands, he encounters Major Sholto – a gambler in debt. Small tempts him with information about the treasure in return for an escape plan. Sholto then leaves the camp and steals the treasure.

Coincidentally, Small is able to save the life of Tonga, an islander. Tonga then helps him to escape by boat and they eventually arrive in England, where Small seeks out Major Sholto. Small then recaps the events that have occurred in the novel so far.

The end of the novel

Jones takes Small into custody, Watson announces his marriage to Mary, and Holmes reaches again for his cocaine.

DO IT!

The 'Strange Story of Jonathan Small' is the longest chapter in the novel, and Holmes hardly features in it. Why do you think Conan Doyle has included this extended first-person account from Small?

Extract 1

Jonathan Small describes his life at the Agra fort.

> 'Well, I was pretty proud at having this small command given me, since I was
> a raw recruit, and a game-legged one at that. For two nights I kept the watch
> with my Punjaubees. They were tall, fierce-looking chaps, Mahomet Singh and
> Abdullah Khan by name, both old fighting-men who had borne arms against us at
> 5 Chilian-wallah. They could talk English pretty well, but I could get little out of them.
> They preferred to stand together and jabber all night in their queer Sikh lingo. For
> myself, I used to stand outside the gateway, looking down on the broad, winding
> river and on the twinkling lights of the great city. The beating of drums, the rattle of
> tomtoms, and the yells and howls of the rebels, drunk with opium and
> 10 with bhang, were enough to remind us all night of our dangerous neighbours
> across the stream. Every two hours the officer of the night used to come round
> to all the posts, to make sure that all was well.'

Although Small began life as 'a bit of a rover', he appears to have been well-intentioned in his working life.

Small is notable for presenting 'foreigners' with some respect.

Conan Doyle builds up a menacing atmosphere using an extended list within this sentence.

It is ironic that Small calls the rebels 'neighbours' as the word has connotations of friendliness.

DEFINE IT!

bhang – a drug, an edible form of cannabis

game-legged – one legged

opium – a chemical used as a drug (from which heroin is produced)

Punjaubees – Punjabis (people from the province of Punjab, India)

The Indian Mutiny

DO IT!

1 In his narrative, Small focuses on his sense of isolation in this foreign land. Find two examples of this isolation.

2 Explain how Conan Doyle creates a sense of fearsome chaos for his reader in the second part of the extract.

Character and theme essentials

This chapter is the longest in the novel and the one in which Holmes features the least. He, Watson and Jones are largely absent until the last two pages. Conan Doyle uses Small's monologue to give historical context and an explanation of the origin of the treasure. However, he could have done so much more economically, so why has he given the character of Small such a substantial platform?

Justice and injustice

Small begins life in a 'steady, chapel-going' family but he gets into trouble and eventually takes 'the queen's shilling' to get out of a 'mess over a girl'. From there, life goes rapidly downhill – he loses his leg to a crocodile, gets caught up in the horrific Indian Rebellion, has to choose between losing his own life or helping to take that of another, then faces jail, escape and ultimately rearrest.

Although Watson 'conceived the utmost horror of the man' and Holmes and Jones share the 'same disgust', it is hard to feel that Conan Doyle actually condemns Small as an evil character. There seems to be some sympathy that he has experienced the accidents of life and did not have the option of another path…until he is consumed with anger at Sholto and attempts to hunt down the treasure.

Notably, Conan Doyle gives these words to Abdullah Khan:

> 'Consider, Sahib,' said he, 'that if this man is taken by the commandant he will be hung or shot, and his jewels taken by the government, so that no man will be a rupee the better for them. Now, since we do the taking of him, why should we not do the rest as well? The jewels will be as well with us as in the Company's coffers.'

It is suggested here that the East India Company is guilty of crimes – but as a 'smaller' person in society, Jonathan Small is easily punished for his crime, whereas more powerful businesses, armies and governments are not. (Perhaps Conan Doyle is condemning the crimes that Small commits, but is giving a balanced view of the man that commits them and the Empire of which he is a part.)

DO IT!

Is Conan Doyle criticising the abuse of power by those in senior roles? Explain your opinion using evidence from the novel.

Honour

Small and his co-conspirators have a defined code of honour and oaths, albeit they are united in crime. Major Sholto, on the other hand, acts dishonourably by taking the treasure for himself and failing to fulfil his promises. He lives a life of fear, unable to enjoy the treasure.

Small is recognised by the colonel (who helps him to get a job after his leg is bitten off) and he is given responsibility in the fort at Agra so he must have some redeeming qualities. He is brutally honest in telling Holmes every detail of his misdeeds. (Although he is the one to be punished at the end of the tale, Small's tale allows the reader to see that there are others equally as dishonourable as Small in this narrative.)

REVIEW IT!

1 What did Small do with the treasure? How does this show he is 'shrewd'?

2 Jones refers to 'justice'. What is Small's reaction?

3 What is 'taking the queen's shilling'?

4 How did Small lose his leg?

5 What does Small become after he recovers? Who recommended him for this? What does that suggest about Small?

6 Select a noun phrase or a selection of adjectives to give an example of the violence from the Indian Mutiny. Why did Conan Doyle describe it so graphically?

7 Find the paragraph beginning, 'The city of Agra is a great place, swarming with fanatics and fierce devil-worshippers…' How does Conan Doyle's choice of language convey chaos here?

8 Jonathan Small describes chaos, trauma and his own isolation. Do you sympathise with him at this point?

9 Small has the safety of the fort as a priority. He also abides by his oath. Do these attitudes make him an honourable character?

10 'We only ask you to do that which your countrymen came to this land for. We ask you to be rich.' What is Conan Doyle's attitude to the expansion of the British Empire here?

11 Oaths, treasure, disguises: what kind of a tale would Mrs Forrester call Small's adventures?

12 Find the paragraph beginning: 'The rain was still falling steadily…' How does the description of the weather echo what is about to happen?

13 Dost Akbar is described as huge and Achmet as small and fat: a 'fat man' chased by a 'bounding… tiger'. Is this description intended to be horrific or comical, or both?

14 The narrative is paused for Small to drink some whiskey. Watson comments on his own 'utmost horror' and Holmes' 'disgust'. Why does Conan Doyle pause the narrative? What is the effect of this on the reader?

15 How does Conan Doyle generate a negative portrayal of Sholto?

16 How is Captain Morstan involved?

17 Does Morstan escape blame from Small?

18 How does Jones add some humour as he takes Small away?

19 What is Holmes' attitude to Watson's intended marriage?

20 Conan Doyle uses the final image of Holmes to give a circular structure to the novel. What is the final image of Holmes and why do you think Conan Doyle chose this?

Characters

Sherlock Holmes

What do we know about Sherlock Homes?

- He is an independent private detective.
- He thrives on the mental stimulation of investigating cases.
- He is highly knowledgeable – about everything.
- He believes in fairness and justice.

Victorian readers may have known of Sherlock Holmes from, *A Study in Scarlet*. Modern readers may have a view of him from other novels and from films. So, the challenge is to focus on what is learned about Holmes in *The Sign of Four*. How does Holmes develop as a character through this novel? Compare Holmes' presentation at the beginning of the novel to his development throughout.

What do you think are the five most important points to remember about Conan Doyle's presentation of Sherlock Holmes?

Find a quotation for each to support your answers. Comment on Conan Doyle's style in each of the quotations.

The first row of the table has been completed as an example, to start you off.

Point about Conan Doyle's presentation of Sherlock Holmes	Quotation	Conan Doyle's style
Sense of humour	'…the dead man very considerately got up and locked the door on the inside.'	The tone is undramatic. It is typical of Holmes' wry comments and his gentle mockery of the police force.

Beginning of the novel	
Characteristic	**Example**
Appearance: 'clear-cut, hawklike features'	He is compared to a bloodhound, a hawk and an eagle – creatures with great 'detecting' abilities.
Addiction: 'innumerable puncture-marks'	Holmes' drug use is presented as a way of making him seem flamboyant and risk-taking, and of emphasising his boredom with ordinary life. A modern interpretation would see this behaviour as symptomatic of a problem, however.
Detached: 'a client is to me a mere unit'	Insensitive: he does not anticipate Dr Watson's distress at discussing his brother, but he apologises immediately on discovering that Watson is upset. He uses 'brisk, business tones' when telling Mary Morstan to state her case. But he is willing to help, and had been recommended by Mary's employer for his 'kindness and skill'.
Analytical, knowledgeable – and arrogant?: 'I never make exceptions.'	He mentions the pamphlets he has published and the commendations he has received. However, this is the start of the novel and Conan Doyle needs to establish that Holmes is knowledgeable and respected.
A believer in justice and equality	Holmes assesses a person's worth according to their actions, not their appearance. He demonstrates this in his example of the 'repellent' philanthropist who does good in comparison to the 'winning woman' who murdered three children.
Communication	Holmes speaks at length and in long, complex sentences in Chapter One, sounding pompous. However, he becomes more direct and uses shorter sentences and simpler vocabulary in the interview with Mary, appearing more approachable.

DO IT!

While waiting to chase the *Aurora*, Holmes says of the working-class people near the river:

" Dirty-looking rascals, but I suppose everyone has some little immortal spark concealed about him…A strange enigma is man! "

1 Does Holmes say this fondly or critically?

2 Is this what really interests Holmes? How does it link to his first comment, 'I cannot live without brainwork'?

3 This phrase indicates that *everyone* is special in some way. What does this suggest about Holmes' attitude?

Later development		
Is Sherlock Holmes…	**Supporting evidence**	**Comment**
…assertive and decisive, or domineering?	He uses imperative verbs to Watson: 'Look here', 'Just sit'	However, his affection for Watson is evident (see below).
	He directs other characters: 'I want one boy to, 'You must be'	However, this fits with their inferior social status.
	Holmes must be 'master' of the plan with Athelney Jones to capture Jonathan Small.	Given Jones' bungling so far, this is a good choice, not arrogance.
…kind and courteous?	Holmes is kind to those more vulnerable than himself.	He helps Thaddeus Sholto despite his unattractive appearance. He anticipates Watson's tiredness when they follow Toby. He understands the growing romance and arranges for Watson to open the treasure with Mary. He generously allows Jones to take credit for his successes, and he recognises that Jones is a worthy collaborator, inviting him for supper. He offers Small a cigar.
…humorous?	In the first chapter, Holmes is found 'chuckling' at Watson. This may seem patronising at first, but can be interpreted more sympathetically after we know Holmes better.	Later, he gives a 'slight smile' at Jones' arrogance and we find him laughing uncontrollably at Toby's mistake. His sense of humour seems well-developed.
…a believer in justice and equality?	Holmes establishes good relations with his social inferiors. Although Victorian conventions place Holmes above them in the social hierarchy, these interactions show him to lack snobbish superiority. Holmes is racist about Tonga. This may be a sign of his times, but a modern reader would be unlikely to forgive him that. Although not a misogynist, he expresses some chauvinism: 'Women are never to be entirely trusted…' Yet, he behaves politely within the conventions of the era.	
…communicative?	Watson notes that Holmes 'could talk exceedingly well'. Holmes uses irony with Jones, dialect with Mrs Smith, good humour with McMurdo. He questions Watson and encourages him to analyse (though this is also a narrative device to allow Holmes to correct him!). He issues instructions and adds urgency during the chase sequence.	

Dr Watson

What do we know about Dr Watson?

- He is a former military doctor who has a wounded leg.

- He is an admiring friend and housemate of Sherlock Holmes.

- He takes part in and narrates events during Holmes' investigations.

- He falls in love with Mary Morstan and proposes marriage to her.

Dr Watson has several functions within the novel. He is the narrator, a foil to Holmes and a romantic hero.

Role	How does this role affect the novel?	Supporting evidence
Narrator	We are presented with Watson's perspective on characters and events.	Watson is powerful as he directs the reader's viewpoint. While being a loyal friend to Holmes, he also criticises and challenges him, though Holmes always turns out to the right in the end. He is also critical of Thaddeus Sholto, Athelney Jones and Jonathan Small, which colours the reader's perception of these characters.
Foil	Watson and Holmes are given characteristics that contrast. This serves to emphasise Holmes' characteristics.	Watson is intelligent – he is a doctor and knowledgeable. Holmes is brilliant – he shows expertise on many topics. Watson is sentimental and, at times, emotional. Holmes can appear cold and is always analytical. Watson will take part in adventurous action. Holmes leads it. Watson is sometimes critical of other characters. Holmes is dispassionate.
Romantic hero	He leads the romantic sub-plot, increasing the appeal to the magazine readership and making the novel multi-dimensional.	Watson's attraction to Mary Morstan breaks up the main detective plot and offers the reader diversion. The reader identifies with Watson while probably admiring Holmes. So, the progress of the relationship allows the reader to see Watson valued and developed – rather than just being a sidekick to Holmes.

DO IT!

Which of the adjectives below would you apply to Watson? Think of an example to support each of your choices.

loyal
considerate
sensitive
daring
tenacious
critical
observant
protective
self-critical
apprehensive
conventional
biased
petty
submissive

Mary Morstan

What do we know about Mary Morstan?

- She is a middle-class lady who is employed as a companion.
- She is an orphan whose father was killed in relation to the Agra treasure.
- She begins the events of the novel through her request for help from Sherlock Holmes.
- She is the object of Dr Watson's affections and she falls in love with him.

NAIL IT!

It will be helpful to your exam analysis if you can make links or comparisons to how characters develop and change, or remain 'fixed' and perhaps stereotyped.

Mary's role is limited, though she has a presence throughout the novel, unlike other minor characters. She moves from being an instigator of action to a receiver of news about events, and of Watson's affections. Watson focuses on Mary's emotional responses to events and she becomes a less precise character and more representative of female 'good'. Her character seems to dissolve rather than develop across the novel.

At first, Mary is an *active* character:
- She presents the problem to be solved.
- She is the focus of Watson's romantic attentions.
- She attends the meeting with Thaddeus Sholto.
- She holds hands with Watson in the garden of Pondicherry Lodge.

She then has a *supportive* role in Chapter Five:
- She comforts the housekeeper at Pondicherry Lodge.

From Chapter Six onwards, she is a *passive* character:
- She weeps in the carriage with Watson.
- She turns white when told of the events of the chase.
- She sits in a state of melancholy at the window.
- She embraces Watson and is happy.

DO IT!

What do these events show you about Mary? Use them to identify the characteristics she shows in the early part of the novel.

- She has come to ask Holmes' advice.
- She states her case clearly and without emotion.
- She attempts to find her father after his disappearance.
- She is prepared – bringing the pearls, and then the Agra note.
- She goes to an unknown house, Pondicherry Lodge, late at night.
- She seems to lack interest in the possibility of money and is more interested in the mystery.
- She thanks Thaddeus when she meets him (and later, is concerned for him after his arrest).

Athelney Jones

What do we know about Athelney Jones?

- He is a police officer already known to Holmes.
- He seems to be rather vain about his abilities.
- He is liked by Holmes, who invites him to dinner.
- He allows Holmes to lead the final chase.

Athelney Jones represents the 'accredited representatives of the law', as Holmes calls the police. His role is to accentuate Holmes' brilliance. He is presented largely as a stock figure of the working-class bumbling policeman, but he is given moments of added characterisation. He has 'twinkling eyes' despite his description as 'red-faced' and 'burly' and being fond of a whiskey. He is shown at supper as a 'sociable soul'. Conan Doyle wishes the reader merely to smile at his vanity, as Holmes does when Jones takes credit for solving crimes.

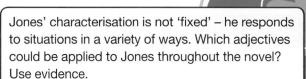

DO IT!

Jones' characterisation is not 'fixed' – he responds to situations in a variety of ways. Which adjectives could be applied to Jones throughout the novel? Use evidence.

arrogant   patronising   good-humoured
bumbling   misguided   stubborn
charming   acquiescent   comic

Thaddeus Sholto

What do we know about Thaddeus Sholto?

- He is the son of Major Sholto, who stole the Agra treasure.
- He is the brother of Bartholomew Sholto, who was murdered for the treasure.
- He shows a sense of fairness to Mary in sending her parts of the treasure.
- He is a fearful and peculiar-looking character.

Thaddeus Sholto is the mysterious benefactor whose note to Mary triggers the whole plot. The son of Major Sholto and the brother of Bartholomew, he is benevolent and they are punished for their greed.

He is presented by Watson as peculiar and slightly unpleasant. He is a hypochondriac and always nervously agitated. He receives a lot of description in comparison with the amount of live action he participates in. He serves to show how doing good will be rewarded and to demonstrate Holmes' and Mary's lack of bias compared to other characters.

Jonathan Small

What do we know about Jonathan Small?

- He was a soldier in the Indian army.
- He lost a leg to a crocodile.
- He stole the Agra treasure in India.
- He has spent much of his life in prison.

Before we meet Jonathan Small, he is described by Holmes as a result of his investigations. His background, beliefs and sense of justice are developed. Conan Doyle placed Small's history at the end of the novel in a long chapter, suggesting that he considered it of interest and significance for his readers.

	How Conan Doyle presents Jonathan Small during the novel
Criticism?	<ul><li>Prior to his narrative, he is presented as a stereotypical villain.</li><li>He is shown to be angry and obsessive.</li><li>He beats Tonga and exhibits him.</li><li>He participates in murdering Achmet, the merchant.</li><li>He kills his guard with his wooden leg.</li></ul>
Redeeming features?	<ul><li>He is respectful to Holmes.</li><li>Holmes recognises that he is 'shrewd'.</li><li>He has remorse for the death of Bartholomew Sholto.</li><li>He makes the best of life after losing his leg.</li><li>He is true to his oath and loyal to his co-conspirators.</li><li>He shows more empathy for Tonga than any other character does.</li><li>He appears to give an honest narrative.</li><li>He was willing to give his life to save women and children at the fort.</li><li>He recognises the power that the treasure has held over them all.</li></ul>

Tonga the Islander

What do we know about Tonga the Islander?

- He is very small, with sharp teeth.
- He is loyal to Jonathan Small.
- He murders Bartholomew Sholto.
- He dies in the waters of the River Thames.

In contrast to Small, Tonga is presented in one-dimension as a caricature of what Victorians may have wanted exotic foreigners to be like. Tonga is described using negative language and racist imagery – 'savage', 'imp', 'devil', 'black fellow' – except by Small, who refers to Tonga's loyalty ('he was staunch and true'). Sometimes their relationship is more like that of master and animal ('he was as venomous as a young snake'). However, Small has a fondness for Tonga: 'my little chum'.

Minor characters of the lower classes

Conan Doyle introduces minor characters to add humour and provide a contrast to the intellectual conversation of Holmes and Watson.

Character	Type of humour	Characteristics
McMurdo	Irony	He is a prizefighter. Initially, he refuses entry to Holmes and Watson, but he knows and respects Holmes.
Mr Sherman, Toby's owner	Slapstick of calling Watson names	He is rude to Watson at first, then polite when he knows he is a friend of Holmes.
Mrs Smith and Jack	Jack's cheekiness	She is unstoppably talkative and indiscreet – telling her worries to a stranger. This would be humorous to a Victorian reader.
Wiggins and the Baker Street Irregulars	Slapstick manner of appearance and disappearance	They enter in organised chaos and all line up in a **parody** of a police parade. Their position is below the working classes (they survive by begging or stealing). However, Holmes harnesses their intelligence and tenacity in his own 'irregular' police force. Ironically, they are trusted and reliable. Wiggins is 'stood forward with an air of lounging superiority which was very funny in such a disreputable little scarecrow.' He is fondly mocked to make the readers smile.

REVIEW IT!

1 Why does Conan Doyle open with the drug-taking moment? How might Victorian and modern readers respond to this scene?

2 Give an example of Holmes' lack of bias about people's appearance.

3 What is a monograph and why is Holmes talking about them?

4 How does Conan Doyle intend the reader to respond to Holmes at first?

5 Is Holmes more of an intellectual than an action hero? Support your opinion with evidence.

6 Does Holmes treat Watson with respect? Support your opinion with evidence from the novel.

7 Summarise Watson's personal history.

8 Why has Conan Doyle added a companion for Holmes to the novel?

9 What is a foil? And is Watson a foil to Holmes?

10 How does Watson differ from Holmes?

11 What might Mary Morstan's virtues be in the eyes of a Victorian reader?

12 How does Mary's view of Thaddeus Sholto differ from Watson's?

13 How does Mary respond to the loss of her potential inheritance?

14 Who lived at Pondicherry Lodge?

15 Who is greedier – Major Sholto or Jonathan Small? Explain your opinion.

16 Why does Holmes want to interview Jonathan Small?

17 Is Conan Doyle completely critical of Athelney Jones? Explain your opinion.

18 Name three of the lower-class characters.

19 How does Conan Doyle mock the police through the Baker Street Irregulars?

20 Are Conan Doyle's characters realistic? Explain your opinion.

Themes and contexts

Empire

Queen Victoria reigned from 20 June 1837 until her death on 22 January 1901. It is known as the Victorian era. It was a long period of peace, wealth and commercial exploration of the wider world to expand the British Empire.

The British Empire grew across the Victorian era. At its most powerful, Britain ruled about a quarter of the world, in terms of both land and population. However, international travel was very limited so most British citizens would not have visited other countries. By 1889, when *The Sign of Four* was published, British people would have been *aware* of other countries in the Empire, but probably did not *know* much about them. They would have felt important to know that their country was a world power. The Empire provided middle-class Britain with impressive luxury (see Bartholomew Sholto's apartment), but also a source of fear of things that they did not understand.

Queen Victoria became Empress of India in 1887 and armed forces would have been in the country before that. Captain Morstan and Major Sholto served in India. The Andaman Islands are remote islands in the Indian Ocean under British rule and were used as a prison for convicts during the Victorian era. They had also experienced violent revolts by the native population, as Holmes finds in his 'gazetteer'.

Battles with overseas places would have been reported in the press, giving the impression that foreigners were dangerous. In 1857 the extremely bloody Indian Mutiny had taken place, as described by Small in the last chapter.

So, Conan Doyle provides the reader with automatic curiosity about the unknown, and excitement at danger by bringing elements from overseas into the story (much as a film set in an exotic location may do for you today, or how certain nationalities rotate as 'baddies' depending upon current political situations).

1 Re-read the description of Thaddeus Sholto's apartment at the beginning of Chapter Four. Select three examples of items that have come from the overseas Empire. Explain the intended effect of these items on a Victorian reader. Would a modern reader's response differ from a Victorian's?

2 Re-read the description of the Agra treasure in Chapter Twelve, beginning 'There were one hundred and forty-three diamonds…' Why do you think Conan Doyle spent so much time focusing on this treasure?

Race

Indian characters who are mentioned in the novel are either servants or assassins. Abdullah Khan, Dost Akbar (referred to as Sikhs though their names are Muslim) and Mahomet Singh, along with Small, are the 'Four' of the title. They are presented as alien by Jonathan Small: 'tall, fierce-looking chaps' who 'jabber…in their queer Sikh lingo'. However, they have their own code of honour and do not betray one another, or him.

Lal Chowdar and Lal Rao (servants brought to England from India) bring exoticism to the novel in the way they dress. They represent deceit, betraying Bartholomew Sholto and covering up the death of Captain Morstan.

The bloody descriptions of the rebellion are gruesome, including 'Dawson's wife, all cut into ribbons', and are brutal for the time in which they are written. They confirm the idea of dangerous 'others' who could harm Britons.

Tonga is presented as even more dangerous, strange and savage, even though he demonstrates loyalty (see page 70 for further consideration of his role).

1 Bearing in mind that he is a product of his time, to what extent would you consider Conan Doyle to be racist in his choices for this novel?

2 Can a modern audience still enjoy this novel with the blatant racism that is presented, particularly in Small's account and in Chapter Ten: The End of the Islander? Write a paragraph explaining your opinion.

Women

Women were perceived to be morally good. Women did not yet have the right to vote (along with many men at this time). Middle-class women were generally dependent upon their husbands or fathers, both financially and for their freedom. Presentations of women in fiction, and the expectations of society, were that a woman should be modest and selfless, and should defer to her husband or father for guidance.

As the key female in the novel, Mary Morstan's role is interesting. She begins with some strength and independence, which is admired by Holmes; at the ending he again compliments her for her 'genius' rather than for her good manners. However, he, too, says that 'Women should not be entirely trusted…' in a very chauvinistic statement. In fact, it is Watson who presents Mary, as the representative female, as becoming weaker and more dependent upon him through the novel. The reader has a challenge in deciding whether this attitude should be attributed to his narrative perspective or whether it is the intention of Conan Doyle to show that women need masculine support and protection.

Detection and science

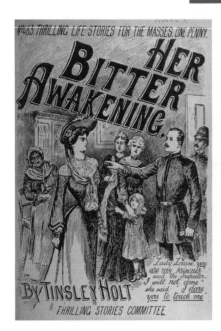

The beginning of the police force, and especially the increase in detection rather than prevention of crime (see page 38), led to a new area of inspiration for narratives and gave birth to the detective fiction genre. The genre began with penny dreadfuls (cheap serialised fiction for the working classes) and made its way across to mainstream middle-class literature. Sherlock Holmes was not the first detective hero from this period of history, but he is the most enduring. Mystery and detection grip readers (and viewers) today, providing suspense, excitement, intrigue and the entertainment of unpicking the clues alongside characters.

Conan Doyle trained as a medical doctor and his interest in analysis is transferred to Sherlock Holmes. Science was making further breakthroughs during the Victorian period and caused great controversy. Some of the new ideas inspired fear among the population, such as using corpses to learn more about anatomy, Darwin's theory of evolution and spiritualism.

Conan Doyle's references to science are very specific and do not upset the accepted order by challenging beliefs about God and creation. Holmes is ahead of his time in using techniques of forensic science such as fingerprint and footprint analysis – these were not adopted by police forces until some time after this novel was published. Holmes also uses systematic observation and experiments to gain expertise on handwriting and tobacco. The contemporary popularity of the Sherlock Holmes stories probably indicates that this science was new and exciting to read about, rather than fear-inspiring.

DEFINE IT!

Darwin's theory of evolution – scientific theory put forward by Charles Darwin (1809–82), which states that living creatures adapt (change) over time

DO IT!

Make a list of the science used by Holmes in this novel. Consider what effect mention of these topics would have had on a Victorian reader. How does a modern reader respond?

Morality and justice

In a moralistic narrative, the characters who do bad deeds are punished or suffer and the good are rewarded in some way. Clearly, detective fiction lends itself to being moralistic because the perpetrators of the crime or misdeed (if the 'bad deed' is not legally a crime) are usually brought to account or punished in some way. Thus, good triumphs over evil.

STRETCH IT!

Is *The Sign of Four* a tale of morality or an entertaining crime story – or both? Explain your opinion using evidence from the novel.

DO IT!

1 Consider the morally just behaviour listed below. Is this action rewarded? Make notes of your evidence.

- Holmes assists Mary Morstan (for no stated personal gain).
- Thaddeus Sholto sends pearls to Mary.
- Holmes will prove Thaddeus Sholto did not steal the treasure.
- Mary is not greedy for money.
- Watson is not a fortune-hunter.

2 Consider the injustices. Is this action punished? Make notes of your evidence.

- Major Sholto has illicit treasure.
- Bartholomew Sholto does not want to share the treasure with Mary.
- Thaddeus Sholto is arrested.
- Tonga murders Bartholomew Sholto.

REVIEW IT!

1 What is the British Empire?

2 What did Britain gain from the Empire?

3 What fears did the Empire bring to middle-class Victorians?

4 How would Victorian people learn about people from other lands?

5 How did Victorians view people of other races?

6 Which character represents 'savagery' in the novel?

7 How significant is it that this character is not named until almost the end of the tale?

8 In your opinion, are Conan Doyle, Holmes or Watson racist in their views? Explain your answer using evidence from the novel.

9 Is Mary presented as a damsel in distress? Explain your response.

10 Whose attitude to women is closest to your own – Holmes' or Watson's?

11 Holmes' use of scientific methods was at the forefront of discoveries during the Victorian era. How might Victorian readers have felt about the descriptions of detective techniques?

12 Holmes' use of trace techniques are known to us today. How does a modern reader respond to Holmes' experiments?

13 Are any of the characters in the novel wholly good or wholly evil? Explain your opinion using evidence from the novel.

14 Jonathan Small is the most morally complex character. Why does Conan Doyle give him the longest chapter?

15 Is Conan Doyle a believer in social equality? Explain your opinion using evidence from the novel.

16 Is Holmes characterised as a snob? Give reasons.

17 Is Conan Doyle fair in his presentation of the police force? Explain your view.

18 Why do you think Conan Doyle placed the narrative within the context of the Indian Mutiny?

19 In what ways might this novel be considered a perfect detective story? Explain your opinion using evidence from the novel.

20 Is this Sherlock Holmes story still relevant today? Explain your opinion using evidence from the novel.

Language, structure and form

NAILIT!

Check that you understand the terminology for discussing sentence structures: rhythm, repetition, listing, extended phrases, rhetorical questions, statement instruction, exclamation.

Language: Sentence structures and language choices

As all writers do, Conan Doyle chooses the length, structure and type of sentence to support what he wants to convey to the reader.

What impression do you get of Holmes' mood and behaviour? How do the language choices support that impression?

What is the effect of repeating the 'hard' sounding 'what'?

What impression do these colours create?

> …I cannot live without brainwork. What else is there to live for? Stand at the window here. Was ever such a dreary, dismal, unprofitable world?
> 5 See how the yellow fog swirls down the street and drifts across the dun-coloured houses. What could be more hopelessly prosaic and material? What is the use of having
> 10 powers, doctor, when one has no field upon which to exert them? Crime is commonplace, existence is commonplace, and no qualities save those which are commonplace have
> 15 any function upon earth.

What is the effect of questions, rather than statements?

What is the effect of Conan Doyle's verb choices?

How does repeating 'commonplace' emphasise the meaning of the word?

NAILIT!

You may have to look quite carefully for commonplace metaphorical language to analyse, so take your time.

Metaphor and simile

Like most writers, Conan Doyle uses metaphor and simile, but they are often quite commonplace comparisons.

- Holmes is hawklike, like a bloodhound, and aquiline.

- Mary is angelic, treasure, and the golden barrier between her and Watson is removed.

- Thaddeus Sholto's bald head is 'like a mountain-peak from fir-trees'.

DEFINEIT!

aquiline – like an eagle

Alliteration and other sound effects

A writer may choose to group words with similar sounds to create an effect by:

- emphasising the meaning of the phrase
- recreating the emotional content of the words
- recreating the sounds that the words describe.

> ...yet I am ashamed to say that selfishness took me by the soul, and that my heart turned as heavy as lead within me. I...sat downcast, with
> 5 my head drooped, deaf to the babble of our new acquaintance. He was clearly a confirmed hypochondriac, and I was dreamily conscious that he was pouring forth interminable
> 10 trains of symptoms, and imploring information as to the composition and action of innumerable quack nostrums, some of which he bore about in a leather case in his pocket.

Sibilance (repetition of 's' sound) emphasises Watson's dramatic sentimentality in saying that his whole soul is overcome with selfishness.

The alliteration of the 'h' sounds are almost like a sigh when said aloud, reflecting how Watson feels.

The alliteration of the heavy 'd' sounds also echo Watson's downcast mood.

NAILIT!

Make sure you understand the terminology with which to discuss sound: alliteration, **sibilance**, assonance, consonance, onomatopoeia.

DOIT!

Look at the green highlight. How does the structure of the long final sentence of this extract support its meaning?

Elevated language

Victorian vocabulary choices are different from our own current expression, and they do sound more formal. However, Holmes, in particular, prefers to use less familiar words for theatrical effect. Here, he is basically saying that he doesn't like to be bored.

> (1) 'My mind,' he said, 'rebels at stagnation. Give me problems, give me work, give me the most abstruse cryptogram or the most intricate analysis, and (2) I am in my own proper atmosphere. I can dispense then with artificial stimulants. But I (3) abhor the dull routine of existence. (4) I crave for mental exaltation.'

DOIT!

1 Match up the examples underlined on the left with their more mundane meanings:
  a I hate daily routine.
  b I am content.
  c I need something to think about.
  d I don't like being bored.

2 What impression is given of Holmes through the vocabulary he uses?

Bear in mind that Conan Doyle needed to hook and entertain readers of a magazine in instalments, not all at once.

Structure: Overview of structure

A variety of techniques vary the plot structure in order to entertain and surprise a reader:

Plot	A typical structure: problem – detection – climax – resolution – exposition
Sub-plot	Sometimes the romantic sub-plot is placed in primary focus.
Introduction of characters	The main characters are introduced early in the novel. Conan Doyle continues to 'inject' variety and entertainment throughout with characters who only appear for short specific scenes. For example, the Baker Street irregulars offer a new point of focus, and temporarily delay the pursuit of Jonathan Small.
Cliffhangers	Some of the chapters end with a hanging question, e.g. at the end of Chapter One, a new person arrives at Baker Street. The reader is curious about her and why she is there.
Texts within the novel	Letters and newspaper reports vary the delivery of information.
Dialogues	Watson narrates overall, but dialogue and monologue are used to insert different voices.
Humour	Comic moments regularly occur, to vary a reader's emotional responses and make the narrative feel lively.
Tension	The tension of suspense (what will they find through the keyhole?) and the tension of excitement (the dog chase and the boat chase) are both used.
Anticlimax	The reader follows Toby through the streets in a rapid sequence that builds tension and expectation of the discovery of Jonathan Small. There is a moment of anticlimax when Toby initially loses the scent, but then the chase is on again. However, the expected climax is **comically deflated** when Toby arrives at the timber-yard and Holmes and Watson fall into laughter.
Hiatus	In order to tease the reader, Holmes sometimes just changes the subject or asks Watson to think about a problem for himself. This creates a pause – a hiatus – in the plot, which inevitably increases the reader's anticipation of the next discovery.

DO IT!

1 How does Conan Doyle build tension throughout the novel? Consider how he uses mystery, suspense and pursuit sequences. Find an example of each. What is the intended effect of these different techniques on the reader?

2 Compare how a Victorian and a modern reader may respond to the romantic sub-plot, given the influences and expectations of their eras.

Contrast and juxtaposition

Be a language detective and look out for contrasting elements in Conan Doyle's descriptions.

As though he is leaving a clue to be noticed by the reader, Conan Doyle will offer a series of observations about a character, but then introduce a detail that seems at odds with the others. This helps to give a sense of unpredictability to characters – as the reader has to wait to see why that detail has been included.

Athelney Jones and Jonathan Small are described in unflattering terms, but they both have 'twinkling eyes'. What are the effects of these juxtapositions on the reader?

Athelney Jones	Jonathan Small
"He was red-faced, burly and plethoric, with a pair of very small twinkling eyes which looked keenly out from between swollen and puffy pouches."	"He sat now with his handcuffed hands upon his lap, and his head sunk upon his breast, while he looked with his keen, twinkling eyes at the box which had been the cause of his ill-doings."
Effect	**Effect**
When the reader first meets Jones, he seems unpleasant but his eyes, although 'small', do suggest that there may be some humour or good nature in him.	After reading on, the reader will understand that Small's eyes were 'twinkling' because he had already emptied the treasure from the box.

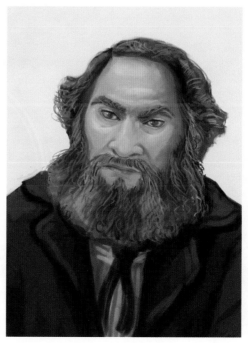

Form

Conan Doyle is a founder of the detective novel form. Many subsequent authors have modelled their work on his form, or intentionally created new variants.

The novel contains three clear parts. In the first part, Holmes is drawn into a mystery – piquing his own and the reader's curiosity. In the second part, there are difficulties that build tension and prevent Holmes from achieving the goal of solving the mystery. In the third part, all the threads of the mystery are resolved – along with those of the sub-plot of Watson's romance.

Narrative voices

One of the strengths of Conan Doyle's novels is the strength of the narrative voices of Holmes and Watson.

Dr Watson

Dr Watson provides the framework narration within which other voices are used. His own narrations have a range of styles:

Author's choice of language	How this language is used by Watson	Example from the text
Precise and observational language	Details of what is seen and heard are precisely recounted. Sometimes he is merely factual.	"Sherlock Holmes took his bottle from the <u>corner of the mantelpiece</u> and his hypodermic syringe from its <u>neat morocco case.</u> The chamber in which we found ourselves was about <u>ten feet one way and six the other</u>."
Figurative language	Watson sometimes includes simile and metaphor, especially when describing Holmes.	"So swift, silent, and furtive were his movements, like those of a trained blood-hound picking out a scent."
Questioning	His questions are used to prompt answers from Holmes.	"'In God's name, what does it all mean?' I asked."
Sentimental language	Each time he mentions Mary, he is swept away with sentiment.	"One white arm and hand drooped over the side of the chair, and her whole pose and figure spoke of an absorbing melancholy."
Evocative language	Watson often adds pathetic fallacy to his descriptions of setting.	"The yellow glare from the shop-windows streamed out into the steamy, vaporous air, and threw a murky, shifting radiance across the crowded thoroughfare."
Melodramatic language	His description of Tonga goes beyond the realistic. It is exaggerated for effect.	"His small eyes glowed and burned with a sombre light, and his thick lips were writhed back from his teeth, which grinned and chattered at us with a half animal fury."
Implicit judgements	Watson is critical in his observations of other characters – particularly Thaddeus Sholto and Jonathan Small.	"Nature had given him a pendulous lip, and a too visible line of yellow and irregular teeth, which he strove feebly to conceal…"

DOIT!

Underline the particular phrases within each quotation that best demonstrate the narrative style identified. The first example has been done for you.

Sherlock Holmes

Sherlock Holmes, too, has a range of styles within his communication.

Author's choice of language	How this language is used by Holmes	Example from the text
Aphorisms	Holmes makes pithy pronouncements – sometimes outrageous ones!	❝'Crime is commonplace, existence is commonplace, and no qualities save those which are commonplace have any function upon earth.' 'Women are never to be entirely trusted, – not the best of them.'❞
Literary allusions	Holmes sometimes adds sayings in French or German.	❝*Schade dass die Natur nur EINEN Mensch aus Dir schuf. Denn zum wuerdigen Mann war und zum Schelmen der Stoff.*❞
Economy	Holmes speaks in long extended sentences about complex matters, but is very economic with words when on the case.	❝'The date?'…'His luggage?' 'No water-pipe near. Roof quite out of reach.'❞
Exposition	Holmes is provided with opportunities to speak and inform the audience of his deductions. On journeys, his knowledge of London instructs the reader about location.	❝'Of course as to his personal appearance he must be middle-aged, and must be sunburned after serving his time in such an oven as the Andamans.' 'Stockwell Place. Robert Street. Cold Harbour Lane.'❞
Imperative	Holmes gives instructions less frequently than may be imagined and usually does so in an understated fashion.	❝'Fire if he raises his hand,' said Holmes, quietly.❞
Ironic	Holmes can be ironic and sarcastic, particularly in relation to the police, but he is not rude.	❝'On which the dead man very considerately got up and locked the door on the inside.' 'Isn't it gorgeous!'' said Holmes, grinning over his coffee-cup.❞
Understated	Adverbs are often used to describe *how* Holmes speaks. His speech is usually quiet and understated.	❝'Oh, this is hardly a case for me to theorize over,' said Holmes, dryly.❞

Victorian readers may have been more aware of Holmes' French and German references. A modern reader would probably have to read a glossary to find out their significance.

NAILIT!

Focus in on short, precise quotations that offer most opportunity for comment.

DOIT!

Consider the reader's reaction to the way Holmes uses language. What judgements do we make about him from his use of language?

Choose one quote at a time. Underline a short selection of words and comment on what they imply about Holmes.

REVIEW IT!

Top up your **subject terminology** by ensuring you know the following terms and can find examples in the novel:

Literary term	Example from the novel	Impact of the language choice in this example
1 Rhetorical question	Holmes is explaining his thinking to Watson: 'Now, what could Jonathan Small do? He could only continue…'	Holmes occasionally uses this device to deliver background information. It makes him sound authoritative and logical. Overuse would make him seem arrogant.
2 Aphorism	'Women are never to be trusted…'	
3 Juxtaposition		
4 Humour		
5 Irony		
6 Sentimentality		
7 Precision		
8 Economy		
9 Imperative		
10 Pathetic fallacy		
11 Alliteration		
12 Simile		
13 Adjectives		
14 Adverbials		
15 Listing within a sentence		
16 Long sentence for effect		
17 Short sentence for effect		
18 Dialect		
19 Exclamation		
20 Elevated language		

Doing well in your AQA exam

Understanding the question

NAIL IT!

- In your AQA exam, the extract will come before the question.
- **Read the question before you read the extract,** so that you read the extract with the question focus in mind.
- Read the question carefully and understand it. Make sure your answer stays relevant to the question.

Make sure you understand the exam question so that you do not include irrelevant material in your answer. Even the extract should be explored *in relation to the question* rather than simply in terms of anything that grabs your attention.

The question below has been annotated by a student so that they fully understand it.

> The extract: I can agree and/or disagree (on one/the other hand).

AQA exam-style question

Starting with this extract, explore how far Conan Doyle presents Holmes as an heroic figure in the novel.

Write about:

- how Conan Doyle presents Holmes in this extract
- how Conan Doyle presents Holmes in the novel as a whole.

> Features of a heroic figure: courage, determination, focus, compassion, perseverance.

> How does he want me to feel about him?

This student has studied the question carefully and realised that:

- the focus is on Holmes as an heroic figure
- 'how far' means the student can agree and/or disagree, or a bit of both
- 'heroic' can be considered from both a Victorian and modern view
- our feelings about Holmes have been controlled by Conan Doyle.

'Pinning the question down' like this – making sure it is fully understood – has allowed the student to then pick out of the extract some useful evidence to support the answer. This provides a starting point from which to consider the rest of the novel.

Choose another question from earlier in this guide. 'Pin the question down' as above.

NAIL IT!

For each paragraph, aim to discuss two or three examples from the rest of the novel in comparison with the example from the extract.

Planning your answer

Once you have made sure you fully understand the question, planning an answer will be quite straightforward. Your brief plan should set out:

- your key, *relevant* ideas
- the content of each of four or five paragraphs
- the order of the paragraphs.

Here is the same student's plan for their answer to the exam question on page 84:

Paragraph	Content		Timing plan
1	Intro - use the question preparation to establish focus of answer		9.40
2	Explore extract - evidence of Holmes' heroic behaviours		9.43
3	Holmes' presentation as detective in the extract and in other parts of the novel	Refer back to extract.	9.58
4	Holmes' presentation as a person in the extract and in other parts of the novel	Refer back to question focus. Question how far 'Holmes is an heroic figure'	10.06
5	Judgement of his failings - from other characters/contemporary reader/modern reader - as presented in this extract and in other parts of the novel		10.14
6	Conclusion - brief return to question		10.22

Sticking to the plan

Note how this student has jotted down time points for when they should move on to the next section of their answer. That way they make sure they do not get stuck on one point and fail to cover the question focus in enough breadth.

Planning to meet the mark scheme

The plan above suggests that the student has thought carefully about the task in the question, that they are familiar with the mark scheme for their AQA 19th-century novel question and are planning to cover its requirements.

Assessment objective	What the plan promises
AO1 Read, understand and respond	Understanding of a number of ideas relevant to the main question focus – likeability, pity for suffering, judgement of failings. Some personal interpretations to be included.
AO2 Language, form and structure	Exploring the extract will ensure close engagement with Conan Doyle's language and structure.
AO3 Contexts	Holmes' rebellion against accepted beliefs of the time. Consideration of how a modern reader may view him – 'how *we* might feel about him'.

(See the summary mark scheme on page 86.)

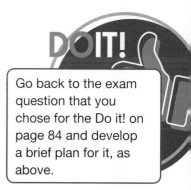

NAIL IT!

In your AQA exam, spend 10–15 minutes on understanding the question and planning your answer. There are no marks for using lots of words. Instead, you should aim to write enough *good, useful* words. Aim for four or five well-planned paragraphs (plus an introduction and conclusion if necessary).

DO IT!

Go back to the exam question that you chose for the Do it! on page 84 and develop a brief plan for it, as above.

What your AQA examiner is looking for

Your AQA examiner will mark your answer according to a mark scheme based on three assessment objectives (AOs). The AOs focus on specific knowledge, understanding and skills. Together, they are worth 30 marks, so it is important to understand what the examiner is looking out for.

Mark scheme

Your AQA examiner will mark your answers in 'bands'. These bands roughly equate as follows:

- band 6 approx. grades 8 and 9
- band 5 approx. grades 6 and 7
- band 4 approx. grades 5 and 6
- band 3 approx. grades 3 and 4
- band 2 approx. grades 1 and 2.

Most importantly, the improvement descriptors below – based on the AQA mark scheme – will help you understand how to improve your answers and gain more marks. The maximum number of marks for each AO is shown.

Assessment objective (AO)		Improvement descriptors				
		Band 2 Your answer…	Band 3 Your answer…	Band 4 Your answer…	Band 5 Your answer…	Band 6 Your answer…
AO1 12 marks	Read, understand and respond Use evidence	is relevant and backs up ideas with references to the novel. makes some comments about these references.	sometimes explains the novel in relation to the question. refers to details in the novel to back up points.	clearly explains the novel in relation to the question. carefully chooses close references to the novel to back up points.	thoughtfully explains the novel in relation to the question. thoughtfully builds appropriate references into points.	critically explores the novel in relation to the question. chooses precise details from the novel to make points convincing.
AO2 12 marks	Language, form and structure Subject terminology	mentions some of Conan Doyle's methods. uses some subject terminology.	comments on some of Conan Doyle's methods, and their effects. uses some relevant terminology.	clearly explains Conan Doyle's key methods, and their effects. helpfully uses varied, relevant terminology.	thoughtfully explores Conan Doyle's methods, and their effects. makes thoughtful use of relevant terminology.	analyses Conan Doyle's methods, and how these influence the reader. chooses subject terminology to make points precise and convincing.
AO3 6 marks	Contexts	makes some simple **inferences** about contexts.	infers Conan Doyle's point of view and the significance of contexts.	shows a clear appreciation of Conan Doyle's point of view and the significance of contexts.	explores Conan Doyle's point of view and the significance of relevant contexts.	makes perceptive and revealing links between the novel and relevant contexts.

AO1 Read, understand and respond/Use evidence

Make sure you read and answer the question carefully. The examiner will be looking for evidence that you have answered the question given. Do not make the mistake of going into the exam with an answer in mind. Knowing the novel well will give you the confidence to show your understanding of the novel and its ideas as you answer the question on the paper in front of you.

Using evidence means supporting your ideas with references to the novel. They can be indirect references – brief mentions of an event or what a character says or does – or direct references – quotations. Choose and use evidence carefully so that it really does support a point you are making. Quotations should be as short as possible, and the very best ones are often neatly built into your writing.

AO2 Language, form and structure/Subject terminology

Remember that *The Sign of Four* is not real life. It is a novel that Conan Doyle has *created* to entertain and influence the audience. The language and other methods he uses have been chosen carefully for effect. Good answers will not just point out good words Conan Doyle has used: they will explore the likely effects of those choices on the audience.

Subject terminology is about choosing your words carefully, using the right words and avoiding vague expressions. It is also about using terminology *helpfully*. For example, here are two different uses of subject terminology; the second is much more useful than the first:

Student answer A

Watson uses the simile 'like a bloodhound' to describe Holmes' behaviour. Holmes is like dog because he can sniff out the clues to find a solution. The simile 'hawklike' also shows that Holmes is good at spotting clues because he looks at things carefully.

Terminology is correctly used.

Direct evidence is relevant.

Implied meaning is recognised.

Student answer B

Watson uses similes to compare Holmes to animals with sharp senses. Holmes is 'like a blood-hound' implying his persistence in hunting down his target. His gaze is 'hawklike', again linking him to hunting and also referring to his detailed visual observations, as seen in the crime-scene analysis at Pondicherry Lodge. The fact that he is compared to animals gives him a practical, physical definition to contrast with his very intellectual side.

Terminology is correctly used.

Implied meaning is explored.

Direct evidence is integrated into explanations.

Link is made to whole text.

AO3 contexts

Context is important when it helps the audience to understand and interpret the meaning and ideas within the novel. Consider how might:

- the society Conan Doyle lived in have influenced his ideas and attitudes?

- the society *you* live in have influenced how *you* respond to ideas and attitudes in the novel?

- knowledge of the whole novel enrich your understanding of the extract?

The best answers will include contextual information that is directly relevant to the *question*, not just the novel. See pages 72–75 for more information and guidance on how to make the most of contexts in your writing.

AO4 Vocabulary, sentence structures, spelling and punctuation

Make sure that you use a range of vocabulary and sentence structures for clarity, purpose and effect. Accurate spelling and punctuation are important too.

NAILIT!

To boost your marks when answering questions, do the following:

- Know the novel well. Read it and study it.
- Don't go into the exam with ready-prepared answers.
- Read the question and make sure you answer it thoughtfully.
- Choose details in the novel that will support your points.
- Don't treat the novel and its characters as though they are real. Instead, ask why Conan Doyle has chosen to create those words or that event. What effect is he trying to achieve?

NAILIT!

Introductions and conclusions need to be useful or they simply waste time. Your opening:

- should be short and relevant
- could introduce a particular angle on the question, or interpretation of it
- could answer the question directly (leaving the rest of the answer to provide supporting detail).

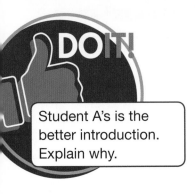

Student A's is the better introduction. Explain why.

Writing your answer

Getting started

Here are the openings of two students' answers to the question we have already looked at on page 84:

Explore how far Conan Doyle presents Holmes as an heroic figure in *The Sign of Four*.

Student answer A

Whether Sherlock Holmes is a heroic figure will depend upon a reader's interpretation of 'heroic' for there are no specific criteria. We could consider whether he is good, whether he is exciting and whether he is noble, but as a heroic detective, he would also need to excel at this. Conan Doyle invites the reader to develop an understanding of Holmes in different situations so our judgement of this character may vary throughout the novel.

Student answer B

I am going to write about how far I agree that Sherlock Holmes is an heroic figure. Clearly, he does good things because he solves the crime and doesn't let people be punished for what they didn't do. However, he has character flaws too. I am going to write about his heroic side and his bad side and make a judgement.

The extract

You do not need to write about the extract and *then* about the rest of the novel. If you feel confident about it, compare the extract with other parts of the novel throughout your answer. However, a safer approach is to begin with the extract and then make connections with other parts of the novel in the following paragraphs. This is the approach suggested in the plan you have already looked at.

Here is part of that student's writing about the extract. Note the way they use the extract to closely examine relevant details of Conan Doyle's language choices. An examiner has made some comments in the margin.

The first time that Holmes is presented as capable in a physically dangerous situation - in the tradition of an action-hero - is when Watson describes him on the roof. Watson uses the simile 'like an enormous glow-worm crawling very slowly along the ridge' to convey how dark the night is, and how Holmes lies prone on the roof top, moving with great care because of the height of the roof. This increases our admiration for Holmes' fearlessness and physical strength, especially as we have been encouraged to think of him as an intellectual character up to this point.

Useful terminology

Effect of words is identified.

Effect explored

Paragraph topics

The rest of your paragraphs should each deal with a sub-topic of the main focus of the question. Here, the question focuses on Holmes as an heroic figure. The student's plan suggests that the next three paragraph topics will be: his heroism as a detective, his heroism as a person, and then judgement of any of his failings. Each of the paragraphs will help the student to address the 'how far' aspect of the question: in other words the student can explore whether Holmes is an heroic figure at a variety of points throughout the novel and in different contexts.

Below you will see how – in this beginning of the 'detective' paragraph – the same student makes references back to both the extract and the question, so as to stay sharply relevant. The references to the question are underlined to point them out.

> In this extract, Holmes is shown to be <u>highly capable, both physically and intellectually.</u> In true detective hero style, he has made his observations and is testing his deductions by 'crawling very slowly along the ridge' and down the 'water-pipe'. In the first chapter, we were introduced to his theory of observation and deduction as the basis for detection. It may be hard for a modern reader to remember that <u>the techniques Holmes uses (such as fingerprint or footprint analysis) were ahead of their times during the Victorian period</u> and didn't become part of police practice until much later. For us today, the techniques seem normal, but it is <u>Holmes' confident use of them and his deductions that continue to impress us. Expertise is an element of heroism within the detective genre.</u>

This student uses **direct evidence** from the extract in the form of a quotation, but also uses **indirect evidence** when referring to another part of the text. Both forms of evidence are valid, but do quote from the extract at least – if only to show you can handle quotations.

Ending your answer

If you write a conclusion, make it useful: don't simply repeat what you have already said. The answer we have been looking at ends with this summary:

> On balance, Holmes is an heroic figure. Being a hero does not mean that a character must be completely without fault. Holmes does, indeed, have character flaws but they are, such as his racism, a product of his time rather than an intended characteristic. As a fictional detective hero he has actually created the model against which others are now measured.

Alternatively, you could remain 'in the balance': you do not have to provide a one-sided agreement or disagreement with the question.

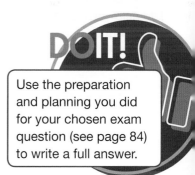

DO IT!

Use the preparation and planning you did for your chosen exam question (see page 84) to write a full answer.

STRETCH IT!

Develop a range of evaluative vocabulary. Use words like:
- condemns
- criticises
- exposes
- ridicules
- subverts
- questions

Going for the top grades

Of course you will always try to write the best answer possible, but if you are aiming for the top grades then it is vital to be clear about what examiners will be looking out for. The best answers will tend to:

• show a clear understanding of both the novel *and* the exam question	**AO1**
• show insight into the novel and the question focus	
• explore the novel in relation to the focus of the question	
• choose evidence precisely and use it fluently	
• analyse Conan Doyle's methods and their effect	**AO2**
• use relevant, helpful subject terminology	
• explore aspects of context that are relevant to the novel and the question.	**AO3**

A great answer **will not** waste words or use evidence for its own sake.

A great answer **will** show that you are engaging directly and thoughtfully with the novel, not just scribbling down everything you have been told about it.

The best answers will be RIPE with ideas and engagement:

R	• Relevant	Stay strictly relevant to the question.
I	• Insightful	Develop relevant insights into the novel, its characters and themes.
P	• Precise	Choose and use evidence precisely so that it strengthens your points.
E	• Exploratory	Explore relevant aspects of the novel, looking at it from more than one angle.

Below is a small part of a student's answer to the question about how far Holmes is an heroic figure.

An examiner has made some comments in the margin.

> Holmes regularly shows respect for specific skills of others, as he does here when he comments 'Confound the fellow!' in surprise at how anyone could have safely climbed down from the roof. Even though he later makes an outrageous comment about women not being 'to be entirely trusted', Holmes does respect Mary and compliments her for the skills he values, calling her a 'genius'. He also recognises that Small is 'shrewd', especially for an uneducated person. It would be easy to dwell on Holmes' comments that seem so politically incorrect to a modern reader, and fail to recognise the personal generosity of spirit that may also be shown. So, if heroes are allowed to have some faults, I feel that Holmes' virtues outweigh his vices.

Clear and **nuanced** point.

Precise choice of evidence.

Precise evidence neatly integrated into **argument**.

Original insight based on context.

Good return to question focus to maintain relevance.

DO IT!

Find an essay or practice answer you have written about *The Sign of Four*.

Use the advice and examples on this page to help you decide how your writing could be improved.

REVIEW IT!

1 What should you do before you read the extract from the novel?

2 Why should you do that before reading the extract?

3 How long should you spend on understanding the question and planning the answer?

4 What three things should be covered in your plan?

5 Why is it helpful to build timings into your plan?

6 How many paragraphs is a good number to plan for?

7 Why is it useful to know the mark scheme?

8 Should you write an introduction and a conclusion?

9 Do you have to write about the extract before writing about the rest of the novel?

10 What should each paragraph of your answer be about?

11 Must you quote from the extract?

12 What is meant by 'evidence'?

13 What should be the focus of your revision in the final month?

14 It is vital that your answer is relevant. Relevant to what?

15 What four ideas should be kept in mind when trying to write a top grade answer?

16 Should you write an introduction to your essay?

17 What is the function of an introduction?

18 What is the function of a conclusion?

19 Why is this a bad conclusion to an answer?

> So that is what I think - Watson is the opposite kind of person to Holmes. I think I've made it clear why.

20 Why is this a better conclusion?

> Overall, Watson and Holmes are characterised differently, though to say that they are opposites may be extreme. They share some characteristics - curiosity, determination, a sense of justice. On the other hand, their analytical skills, relationships and attitudes to social conventions are quite different. This subtlety makes for a better novel than simple, direct contrasts.

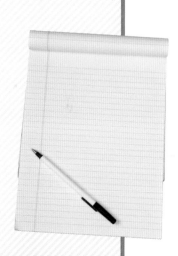

NAIL IT!

In the month leading up to the exam, all your revision should be based on planning and writing answers to exam questions. You will find plenty of exam questions in this guide for practice.

AQA exam-style questions

On these pages you will find two practice questions for *The Sign of Four*. Self-assessment guidance is provided on the app/online. In the exam you will only get one question on this text: you will not have a choice of questions.

NAILIT!

- The question comes immediately after the extract.
- Read the question first.
- Make sure you read the extract with the question in mind.

PRACTICE QUESTION 1

'Justice!' snarled the ex-convict. 'A pretty justice! Whose loot is this, if it is not ours? Where is the justice that I should give it up to those who have never earned it? Look how I have earned it! Twenty long years in that fever-ridden swamp, all day at work under the mangrove-tree, all night chained up in the
5 filthy convict-huts, bitten by mosquitoes, racked with ague, bullied by every cursed black-faced policeman who loved to take it out of a white man. That was how I earned the Agra treasure; and you talk to me of justice because I cannot bear to feel that I have paid this price only that another may enjoy it! I would rather swing a score of times, or have one of Tonga's darts in my
10 hide, than live in a convict's cell and feel that another man is at his ease in a palace with the money that should be mine.' Small had dropped his mask of stoicism, and all this came out in a wild whirl of words, while his eyes blazed, and the handcuffs clanked together with the impassioned movement of his hands. I could understand, as I saw the fury and the
15 passion of the man, that it was no groundless or unnatural terror which had possessed Major Sholto when he first learned that the injured convict was upon his track.
'You forget that we know nothing of all this,' said Holmes quietly. 'We have not heard your story, and we cannot tell how far justice may originally have
20 been on your side.'
'Well, sir, you have been very fair-spoken to me, though I can see that I have you to thank that I have these bracelets upon my wrists. Still, I bear no grudge for that. It is all fair and above-board. If you want to hear my story I have no wish to hold it back. What I say to you is God's truth, every
25 word of it.'

Starting with this extract, explore how Conan Doyle presents the theme of justice in the novel.

Write about:

- how Conan Doyle presents the theme of justice in this extract
- how Conan Doyle presents the theme of justice in the novel as a whole.

[30 marks]

PRACTICE QUESTION 2

'Au revoir,' said our visitor, and, with a bright, kindly glance from one to the other of us, she replaced her pearl-box in her bosom and hurried away. Standing at the window, I watched her walking briskly down the street, until the grey turban and white feather were but a speck in the sombre crowd.

5 'What a very attractive woman!' I exclaimed, turning to my companion. He had lit his pipe again, and was leaning back with drooping eyelids. 'Is she?' he said, languidly. 'I did not observe.' 'You really are an automaton – a calculating-machine!' I cried. 'There is something positively inhuman in you at times.'

10 He smiled gently. 'It is of the first importance,' he said, 'not to allow your judgement to be biased by personal qualities. A client is to me a mere unit, a factor in a problem. The emotional qualities are antagonistic to clear reasoning. I assure you that the most winning woman I ever knew was hanged for poisoning three little children for their insurance-money, and the

15 most repellent man of my acquaintance is a philanthropist who has spent nearly a quarter of a million upon the London poor.' 'In this case, however—' 'I never make exceptions. An exception disproves the rule.'

Starting with this extract, explore how Conan Doyle presents attitudes to women in the novel.

Write about:

- how Conan Doyle presents attitudes to women in this extract

- how Conan Doyle presents attitudes to women in the novel as a whole.

[30 marks]

Glossary

analogy A comparison between two things.

antagonist A **character** who works in opposition to the protagonist (the main character). For example, a villain (antagonist) works against a hero (protagonist).

anticlimax An event that doesn't fulfil a reader's expectations. For example, expectations of excitement or danger are replaced with a comic event.

aphorism A saying that makes a sharp observation about the world.

argument A point of view that is explained and defended. An argument in a text might be a writer's exploration of both sides of a point of view.

character A person in a play or story: a person created by the writer.

chronology The arrangement of events in the order of their time of occurrence.

climax The turning point or most exciting part of the narrative; the point towards which the **plot** has been building, for example, the capture of the criminals.

colloquial language Informal language that is normally used in speech rather than writing (for example: *They're out* rather than *They are not at home*; *yeah* rather than *yes*).

comically deflated Tension is reduced with humour.

connotation The implied (see **implicit** also) meaning of a word or phrase. It is sometimes called a **nuance**. For example, the word *mob* means a large group of people, but it *connotes* violence. If someone *dashes* down the road, we know that they are moving quickly, but that choice of word also *connotes* urgency.

consonance Consonant letters used within and across words for literary effect.

context The set of conditions in which a text was written. These might include: the writer's life; society, habits and beliefs at the time of writing; an event that influenced the writing; the genre of the writing. It is also seen in terms of influences on the reader.

deduce To work something out for yourself, using clues.

dialogue The words that **characters** say in plays or in **fiction**. In fiction, these words are usually shown within quotation marks ('…').

didactic In the **context** of this *Study Guide*, this means informative or instructive.

elevated vocabulary Language outside usual formal use (sometimes to show intellect…or to show off!).

evidence Details or clues that support a point of view. A **quotation** can be a form of evidence in which a few words are copied from a text to support a point of view.

explicit Explicit information is clearly stated; it's on the surface of a text and should be obvious.

exposition An explanation.

fiction Novels or stories made up by an author.

foil In this **context**, a **character** used to contrast and emphasise the qualities of another character.

framed Made distinct; drawn attention to.

Gothic fiction A genre of literature and film that combines **fiction** and horror, death, and at times romance.

hiatus A pause in continuity of a sequence or activity in which nothing happens or is said.

imagery The 'pictures' a writer puts into the reader's mind. Similes and metaphors are particular forms of imagery (see **metaphor** and **simile**). We also talk about violent, graphic, religious imagery, and so on.

implicit (imply) Implicit information is only suggested (or implied), it is not stated directly; we have to **infer** to understand it. The opposite of **explicit**.

infer (inference) To 'read between the lines'; to work out meaning from clues in the text. See **implicit**. When we infer, we are making an inference.

interpret To work out meaning, using clues and **evidence**. The same piece of writing can be interpreted in different ways, but evidence has to support interpretations.

ironic Happening in a way contrary to what is expected, and typically causing some amusement because of this.

irony Mild sarcasm. A **technique** sometimes used by writers to mock a **character** and make them appear ridiculous or dishonest.

language (choices) The words and the **style** that a writer chooses in order to have an effect on a reader.

linear narrative The order in which events are presented corresponds to the order in which they happen.

metaphor A comparison of one thing to another without the use of *like* or *as* (for example: His face *was a thunder cloud*. The boy *was an angry bear*).

monologue A spoken account delivered by one **character**.

narrative device/strategy A method the author uses to present the story.

narrator The **character** who tells the story.

naturalistic A **style** that creates an impression of real-life or being realistic.

noun phrase A group of words built round a noun. In the phrase the noun is the 'head word'.

nuance Implied meaning: see **connotation** and **implicit**.

parody A spoof or imitation of something in order to make fun of it.

pathetic fallacy A term to describe the giving of human emotion and behaviour to nature, for example, landscape. It can be used to imply the emotions of a **character**.

perspective Another term for **viewpoint**. Our perspective is how we 'see' things.

plot The plot of a literary text is the *story* – the narrative – or an interrelated series of events as described by the author.

quotation A word, phrase, sentence or passage copied from a text, usually used to support an **argument** or point of view. A quotation should be surrounded by quotation marks ('…'). It is usually wise to make quotations as short as possible; sometimes just one well-chosen word is enough.

real time The actual time during which a series of events occur.

reflective commentary Thoughts about events or possibilities.

resolution The outcome of the **plot**.

rhetorical question A question in a text, or particularly in speech, for which no answer is expected (for example: *How many times do I have to tell you?*).

sentence structure The grammatical construction of a sentence.

setting The setting is the *time and place* in which a play or story takes place. The setting could also include the social and political circumstances (or **context**) of the action.

sibilance The 's' sound repeated within and across words for literary effect.

simile Comparing two things using either the word *like* or *as* (for example: The boy was *like an angry bear*. His running was *as loud as thunder*; Her face was *as yellow as custard*).

structural device A feature used by a writer to give their writing shape and coherence. They include: **tone**, **style**, repetitions, extended images, shifts of focus, voice and **viewpoint**, openings and closings, sequencing of ideas, links between paragraphs and sentences.

structure How a text is organised and held together: all those things that shape a text and make it coherent.

style Writing styles can vary between writers, or writers may use different styles at different times. Style and **tone** are closely related.

subject terminology The technical words that are used for a particular subject. All the words in this glossary are subject terminology for English Literature.

sub-plot A part of a narrative that develops separately from the main narrative.

technique Another word for method. Writers use different techniques to create different effects.

theme A theme is a central idea in a text. Common themes in writing include: loyalty, love, race, betrayal, poverty, good versus evil, power.

tone The mood of a text, or the attitude of the author or **narrator** towards the topic. Tones can be mocking, affectionate, polite, authoritative, and so on.

viewpoint A writer's or **character's** point of view: their attitudes, beliefs and opinions.

visual Can be 'seen' in your imagination through the description.

vocabulary The words a writer chooses to use. They might use a particular sort of vocabulary (for example: formal, simple or shocking).

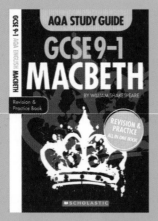

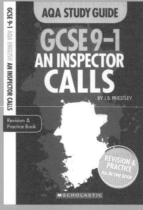
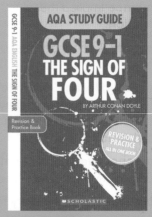

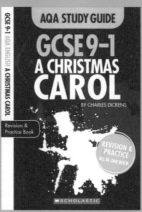
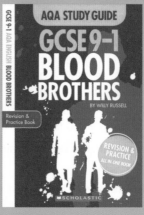